Praise for Rollercoaster

Politicians and other decision makers often have good policy ideas and then leave the room. The rest is left to policy officers who then make the magic happen. Traps to avoid, opportunities to explore, and outcomes to deliver. This book has it all.

Salli Cohen has applied her years of policy expertise and experience to this book.

For those who have just hopped on the policy train as well as for those stuck at a station, *Rollercoaster* is an invaluable resource. Read it, and it will help you help others make a difference.

Jodeen Carney, Commissioner for Equal Opportunity, South Australia

Rollercoaster is a policy bible. Salli Cohen writes in a way that is accessible to all and includes valuable sections at the end of each chapter with key takeaway messages and calls to action. Not only should this book be sitting on every public servant's desk, but it should also be on the desks of those new to policy, those on the frontline of designing and drafting policy and those on the receiving end of policy, implementation and evaluation. I can also see this as a valuable teaching resource for students of public policy.

Dr Lorraine Cherney, Deputy Director Regulatory Practice, ANZSOG

Reading *Rollercoaster* is like having a conversation with a mate who happens to be *bloody good* at policy. Every time I hear the word policy, I think of Salli Cohen and how she makes the subject so straightforward and attainable for even those of us who tremble before the word. Now her knack for simplifying such a complex context has been put to paper, and it reads just as easily.

Cristina (Tina) Da Silva-Cruz, BD / Director,
Konnecto Employment Agency

Many years ago, I would have rolled my eyes and said poolliicy! Now I know that all leaders need to both understand the value of policy and make sure their policy staff have all the support and guidance they need. Thank goodness for this book, which should be included in all leadership programs. I'm so pleased that Salli Cohen has put her knowledge on paper for us all to access.

Annette Gillanders, Director, Biznorth Pty Ltd

I had the privilege of working alongside Salli Cohen during my career in the public service and I am continually inspired by her dedication, intelligence and passion for excellence. *Rollercoaster* is an insightful exploration of the challenges and opportunities in modern policy-making. Cohen's ability to craft such an incredible policy bible, which demystifies the complexities of policy writing and equips the reader to write effective and impactful policies, is brilliant! *Rollercoaster* is a valuable addition to any policy professional's library, an indispensable resource for anyone committed to the craft of policy making, and a *must* for both aspiring and experienced policy writers so they can become *bloody good* ones!

Lidia Di Lembo, Founding Director/Chairperson, SabrinasReach4Life

Rollercoaster draws on the extensive experience of a wonderful policy maker — I can say this, as I was privileged to be Salli Cohen's boss, and observed her in action. Throughout the book, Cohen draws on her experience of policy development, its purpose, the process of development, the varied environments and their outcomes, and the need for regular evaluation.

This is not a dull how-to policy manual. Rather, Cohen drops in large dollops of wisdom, evidence and experience, guiding and challenging us along the roundabout process of policy in its different settings.

The clarity of her writing is a delight, infusing policy with connection, compassion and humanity. I urge you to grab a copy of this book, which will change how you feel about policy. It knocks the dust off a myriad of lever-arch folders and reminds us that policy can change how we work for the betterment of many. Connected and considered policy is a change agent!

Dr Maggie Jamieson

In *Rollercoaster*, Salli Cohen shares the invaluable skills and knowledge she has cultivated throughout her career. She takes the reader on a journey of recognition and discovery, highlighting the intricacies of policy development and the crucial role of policy and policy officers. The book is not only easy to read but also provides actionable guidance for new and experienced policy officers on their journey to becoming *bloody good* policy officers.

I look forward to revisiting this insightful resource regularly.

Associate Professor Nicole O'Reilly, Head of School Allied Health Sciences, Charles Darwin University

We all know there are no silver bullets in the game of policy. But in *Rollercoaster*, Salli Cohen dishes up hidden gems, golden insights and glowing opportunities.

Rollercoaster is an easy-to-read "toolbook" full of little (and big) hints and useful references in a page-turning, clear and straight-talking approach. You can tell that Cohen's tried and tested principles and methods have clearly been used under the blowtorch of policy reality. Yet they are smart and user-focussed, and come with your favourite warm drink and biccies.

Wherever you are in the policy mixmaster, Cohen's *Rollercoaster* will take your ongoing quest to be a *bloody good* policy officer — or in my case, a *bloody good* chair of a community not-for-profit — and help you get there using *bloody good* policy.

Chris Capper, Chair Castlemaine State Festival

A brilliantly upbeat and practical guide to shaping policy that matters. Packed with engaging real-world examples and sharp insights, Salli Cohen breaks down complex concepts with ease and offers a clear, step-by-step approach to modern policy making. Whether you're a beginner or an expert, this accessible and impactful read will leave you feeling confident and inspired, and equip you to make a real difference.

Dr Ben Scambary, Chief Executive Officer, Aboriginal Areas Protection Authority

This book is a reminder that the best communicators make the complex seem simple. Salli Cohen cares about what works, which is why wherever you look, you will see plain English and strong values, with integrated implementation and evaluation. She writes with total street cred, having walked the policy walk in numerous and diverse settings. Policy matters to Cohen because people and justice matter to her.

This is an entirely engaging and entertaining piece of work, and a substantial contribution that, like the rest of her career, makes a real difference.

Enjoy the word pictures and quotable quotes, which you WILL be telling your colleagues about for the longest time.

Craig Kelly, CEO, AnglicareNT

I am gobsmacked by this little beauty! It invoked joy, oozed passion, and is full of *bloody good* tips — sensible stuff that I've already applied (and I'm not even a policy officer!). Salli Cohen brings a combination of humour and smarts to *Rollercoaster* that is innately her. It is as compelling as good fiction, and so remarkably valuable to us all doing good work, whatever that work may be.

Finally, a policy book that made me giggle. I can't believe Cohen essentially brought me to an understanding of the Constitution and the Westminster system when I wasn't even keen — just like that! *Rollercoaster* is a marvellous, funny, valuable book that will help us all do better work.

Ali West, Director, Vibrant Frog, Certified B Corporation

We started our new Public Policy postgraduate degree in 2015 because we knew that policy work in the north of Australia and our near neighbours overseas needed a different approach. The context here in the north is, of course, constrained by the nature of public governance, but it is so different from the policy landscape in Canberra and the southern states.

Policy work here requires you to think on your feet and understand the different cultural and fiscal environments of policy work in smaller and culturally different and diverse places. What a breath of fresh air it was when Salli Cohen began working with us to shape and grow our policy students into '*bloody good*' policy officers. She brought a depth of experience in the nuts and bolts of policy work that nicely balanced the theoretical and philosophical underpinnings we drew from to develop the skills of policy workers in this region and she continues to shape the way we educate our students.

Rollercoaster is more than a breath of fresh air! It is a distilled essence of Salli Cohen, the *bloody good* policy officer. It is set to be a pre-requisite text for our students as we aim to prepare them for the work of making good policy decisions, the work of getting back on their feet, dusting themselves off and keeping on trying when things don't work out.

Salli's wisdom and profound practical insights won't stop policy work from being a rollercoaster, but it will certainly help you enjoy the ride and encourage you to be as passionate about policy work as Salli and our Public Policy team here at Charles Darwin University. Get in touch with Salli and stay in touch! She will be an enthusiastic and staunch supporter of you as you develop your career.

I commend this book to you, and I encourage you to keep it handy. It is set to be one of those books that will become dog-eared, coffee-stained and much loved.

Professor Ruth Wallace, Pro Vice-Chancellor of the Faculty of Arts and Society, Charles Darwin University

Rollercoaster

How to be a *bloody good* policy officer

SALLI COHEN

First Published by Salli Cohen Consulting ABN 67660743877

First edition

Paperback ISBN: 978-1-922740-21-2
Hardcover ISBN: 978-1-922740-24-3
Ebook: ISBN 978-1-922740-23-6

Book Cover by Alice Cohen Design
Illustrations by Alice Cohen Design
Text design and typesetting by Old Mate Media

NATIONAL LIBRARY OF AUSTRALIA   A catalogue record for this book is available from the National Library of Australia

Congratulations

Let me know that you have your copy of *Rollercoaster*. You can:

- DM me on LinkedIn:
  https://www.linkedin.com/in/salli-cohen-the-policy-room/
- Email me: sallicohen@thepolicyroom.com

I can't wait to hear from you.

Acknowledgement of Country

I pay my respect to Larrakia Elders past, present and emerging and to their amazing Larrakia Country where I live, work and play, and where I have written this book. I also pay my respects to First Nations Elders past, present and emerging across Australia.

I extend my deep gratitude to the extraordinary gift of *Makarrata* that has been offered to all Australians through the Uluru Statement from the Heart to "bring us together after a struggle, so that we can face the facts of wrongs and live together in peace".[1]

Dedication

To Wox, I wish you were here.
To Jean, Tom and Alice, you are my everything.

Everyone in this festival is a giver.
Michael Honan, The Festival of Stuff, July 2023 (ABC radio)

Contents

Foreword

As someone who has worked as Salli has, learning on the job about policy — from development to implementation to review and evaluation — I know her book, *Rollercoaster: How to be a bloody good policy officer* could have saved me thousands upon thousands of hours of anguish, self-doubt and lost sleep. If only *Rollercoaster* had been available 35 years ago!

Salli and I met under what could only be described as strange and trying circumstances. Salli was being cross-examined during a hearing of the Royal Commission into the Protection and Detention of Children in the Northern Territory whilst I, as one of the Commissioners, was sitting on the bench watching the hearing unfold. Royal Commissions by nature can be challenging and combative, but I got the sense during her cross-examination that Salli was not your typical bureaucrat. There was something about her composure and confidence under intense questioning. Her evidence was clear, concise and factual, and in our final report, Salli's statements and evidence were extensively cited.

We met again a few years later when I was the CEO of the Batchelor Institute of Indigenous Education and Salli had established The Policy Room, a company that specialises in all aspects of policy. From an awkward first meeting, we became and remain close friends whose conversations will always centre around — you guessed it — policy in all its forms.

From the first chapter, you can tell that Salli is grounded in the daily lives of people working in policy. Who else would have the subtitle *How to be a bloody good policy officer* but someone who gets to the nuts and bolts of policy making? *Rollercoaster* explores the complexities of policy, detailing aspects such as biases and assumptions as well as the importance of providing robust, fearless and candid policy advice to the higher-ups within the Australian system of government.

This book also speaks to the conundrum of policy and decision making as evidenced-based or evidence-informed. As someone who has headed up a research organisation and worked at a senior level of government, I would love for all policies to be evidenced-based. However, because humans are involved, the complexities of policy development and implementation dictate that sometimes compromises must be made. As Salli puts it: "Evidence-informed, while using the best evidence, also includes professional judgement and expertise, including lived experience, context and values. She goes on to say: Evidence-informed policy practice is what *bloody good* policy officers do."

Another thing aspiring *bloody good* policy officers should do is grab a copy of *Rollercoaster* and keep it by their side at all times.

I thank Salli for this book and for using language that makes it accessible and useful to not only us hardcore policy nerds but also to everyday people who can come away with a better understanding of how governments work through the development and implementation of policies.

Mick Gooda
Former Aboriginal and Torres Strait Islander Social Justice Commissioner
Australian Human Rights Commission

Introduction

I have a love-hate relationship with policy. I love its first blush of promises of opportunity, change, hope and difference. I hate how it can be divisive, inequitable, unjust, destructive and isolating. Though after nearly 25 years of working in policy, it still quickens my heart, has my head buzzing with ideas, and gets those butterflies tap dancing in my belly. Why? Because policy matters.

I had no awareness of policy at the beginning of my working life. I had a range of jobs working in Sydney, Noumea and France where I also completed an under-graduate degree that had nothing to do with policy. I returned with my family to Australia at the end of the 1990s and walked right into an unexpected career change as a Northern Territory (NT) public servant.

As a rookie public servant, I discovered that policy — and public service protocols and processes — were at times overwhelming and often unnecessarily complicated. I had no idea what policy was or what it was supposed to do. And yet, whether we realise it or not, policy is part of our everyday lives. It influences:

- vaccinations for our kids
- the safety standards at our work sites
- how we can return an online purchase
- when it's time to start those extra health checks
- what films we can watch at the movies (yes, some of us still go to the movies!)
- the roster at the volunteer fire brigade
- what we can and can't access on the internet
- if we can keep a pet snake at home

- how fast we can drive
- if we can have a surrogate baby
- whether our overseas relatives can migrate to Australia
- and countless other things, both big and small, that directly and indirectly affect us.

This book is based on a simple fact: effective policies, the ones that are going to make a difference throughout our lives, are developed by those who understand how to be a *bloody good* policy officer and how to do *bloody good* policy work.

It took me a long while to work out how to be a *bloody good* policy officer. I made lots of mistakes. (To be fair, I had no idea what I was doing at first, so mistakes were easy.) Nevertheless, I started to grasp the work of a *bloody good* policy officer through my own trial and error.

However, trial and error is inefficient if it's the only avenue to build an expertise. What I needed when I started out was 1) training in policy development, 2) a policy coach and 3) a book that wouldn't fry my brain — specifically, a book that would help me:

- declutter my misconceptions of and assumptions about policy
- unravel the complexity of policy
- learn about policy and its development through real stories and experiences
- gather tools, tips and guidance to pop into my policy kitbag
- to get excited about riding the policy rollercoaster — and to have the courage to hold on tight when I found myself hanging upside down in the carriage, slipping from beneath the seatbelt.

This book is written to accompany you on your journey to become a *bloody good* policy officer. I want you to have the stuff I didn't at the beginning of my policy career, which was:

- a definition of policy as well as of the different policy types and policy development
- an understanding of the system we work in
- an appreciation of the relationship between policy, legislation and regulation (it's not what I thought it was at the beginning of my policy career!)
- insights into how to be a *bloody good* policy officer
- some great tools to get you doing *bloody good* policy work.

Rollercoaster is a curated policy tasting platter just for you.

Who is this book for?

Rollercoaster has been written with the public servant policy novice in mind, regardless of the type or subject matter of the policies you are working on. When I started out in policy, I flew by the seat of my pants; at other times, it was like wading through treacle. What I didn't have was a framework to introduce and guide me through the complex nature and processes of policy development, implementation and evaluation.

The 70-20-10 learning model[1] posits that 70% of our learning is on the job, 20% is through interactions with others and 10% from formal education. In theory, the model makes sense. But when I was starting out, I struggled to identify let alone understand what the policy fundamentals were, and I wasn't learning this on the job. Struggling at the beginning of your policy career isn't necessary — there's no such thing as having to pay your dues before you can do *bloody good* policy work. And that's why I wrote *Rollercoaster* to provide you with the anchor you need to start your policy career and spare you the unnecessary trial and error.

Rollercoaster is also highly relevant to people who work (paid or voluntarily) for organisations such as for-purpose organisations and the private sector whose own policies are influenced by the world of public policy. Or perhaps policy has unexpectedly become part of your life — you might have been asked to write a policy for your kids' sports club. This book is for you too, so keep reading.

How to use this book

Unlike the rollercoaster of policy, there is a logical four-part sequence to this book. Part 1 kicks off with providing you a definition of policy. No more stumbling around on your own in the dark trying to work out what policy is. You will be introduced to the different types of policy — yep, there's more than one. In Part 1 we'll also look at the importance of considering implementation and evaluation at the beginning of every single policy you work on. It's something we policy folk have messed around with for too long, and you can start your policy career on the right foot by making sure implementation and evaluation are not left to the eleventh hour (or the last minute).

A treat awaits you in Part 2 in which you will explore chaos theory firsthand as we examine the delicious contradiction that is the system, aka the beast, aka the machinery of government. Hold on to your bootstraps as we're going to get up close with the Australian Constitution, the Westminster system and the relationship between policy, legislation and regulation.

Part 3 is all about you, about how to be a *bloody good* policy officer. There is a lot more to policy than 'just writing', the common misconception that all you need to do is grab a pen (or a keyboard) and 'write stuff up'. Being a *bloody good* policy officer is so much more than that — and you're going to have to get your head, heart and gut around it.

And last, though certainly not least, Part 4 is all about how to do *bloody good* policy work. In Part 4, I share nine policy tools that I regularly use and that you can put in your policy kitbag to craft the now, to craft what good looks like and to craft the change.

While I'm keen for you to read the whole book, I appreciate that you may want to jump straight to chapters that are going to help you solve the policy conundrums on your desk right now. Maybe your team has a new policy to develop. Perhaps your team is a key partner for another department's policy. Maybe you're identifying stakeholders to be engaged in a policy evaluation. Or you might have been asked to prepare drafting instructions to amend legislation. My advice is that you don't skip chapters 1 to 3. It's important that you understand what policy is, the importance of setting up implementation and evaluation from the get-go, and how to identify and use the different types of policy. Once prepped with these policy fundamentals, sure, take your own journey. Just know that there are valuable policy lessons for you in every chapter.

My hope is that you cover *Rollercoaster* with scribbles and notes, that you turn down the page corners, and that you leave the odd coffee mug stain (even red wine stain, or avocado, spirulina and hemp seed smoothie stain if that's your thing) here and there. My heartfelt apologies to the librarians in my family tree who must be shuddering in their graves. However, if you, dear reader, are doing this, then I know my book is meeting your needs.

Let's get cracking!

Part 1:

What the heck does policy mean?

Some things we wish we knew earlier.
The Imperfects, April 2023 (The Imperfects podcast)

What the heck does policy mean?

Part 1 is about defining policy, with a backstory of my struggles at the beginning of my definition-less policy career! It's important for you to start with three key policy definitions, as I refer to them frequently in this book, and they're going to come up a lot in your work.

Each definition is a piece of the foundational framework you will build to underpin your policy work. Chapter 1 defines policy and clarifies the difference between public policy and 'just' policy. Chapter 2 is all about implementation and evaluation — two critical pieces of policy we must prepare for at the beginning of every policy we work on. Finally, in chapter 3, we consider the different types of policies and how they all come together.

There are two things I want you to keep in mind when considering the policy definitions. First, not everyone will have the same policy or policy-related definitions. Second, always check with other people what their definitions are. Checking gives you an opportunity to get on the same page by coming to a respectful understanding of your differences.* This is more important than haggling over who is right. Checking policy definitions also reduces the risk of a lost opportunity, and mitigates confusion and frustration.

*There is an exception for different policy definitions — the 'public policy' definition is set in stone. More coming up shortly on what public policy is.

For a long time, I couldn't nail a definition of policy that made sense. I found it easier to talk about the policies I was working on rather than turn myself into knots trying to define what seemed undefinable. Policy was, and to this day is, frequently described as a cycle, and this didn't help me either. It made me think of a washing machine, as though I could simply select a cycle and expect the machine to do exactly as it was programmed. Spoiler alert: I have never experienced or seen policy work like this. My experience of policy has been more akin to selecting a setting but having the washing machine change without warning to a different setting and someone throwing their red t-shirt into the white load after I'd already hit the start button.

In the process of writing this book, I spoke with policy colleagues about how to define policy. They confirmed to me that it's something we all struggled with and invariably wished someone had clearly defined for us much earlier in our career. So, if you have been struggling to pin down a definition of policy, you need not feel alone, and you need not wait any longer.

Chapter 1

Kick the policy cycle to the curb — defining policy

What is policy?

Short version: policy is a **change**.

Long version: policy is a **change** that takes **people (or people and things)** from where they are now to where an organisation or a government wants them to be.

There are three components of a policy:

1. The *now* is the starting point.
2. The *what good looks like* is the end point.
3. The *change* happens between the two.

The change a policy invariably creates is a behavioural change.

Regardless of whether a policy is a public policy or not, a policy must be definable, valuable, measurable and implementable (we'll cover this in chapter 2).

Public policy versus policy

The terms public policy and policy are frequently used interchangeably. Rest assured that the definition for policy stands for both public policy and 'just' policy. The difference is that the word 'public' signals a government policy commitment for the people — the public — and is often used when referring broadly to public policies, for example, public education policies, public transport policies or public hospital policies.

The trick — and let's face it, we policy folk are quite the players — is that public policies don't need the word 'public' in their title. Examples of undercover public policies (i.e., no 'public' in their name) include the Koala Conservation Policy,[1] Cruise Ship Operations within the Great Barrier Reef Policy[2] and Competition Manipulation and Sport Wagering Policy.[3] The deadpan title for the latter, however, does give it away as a public policy.

Actually, there is a second trick (I told you, we're quite something): do not automatically assume that policy is only in the government wheelhouse. There are many different types of organisations (for example, for-purpose, non-government, private, volunteer and Aboriginal Community Controlled organisations, among others) and sectors (such as hospitality, arts, recreation and leisure, and construction, to name a few) that have their own policies and policy officers. The more the merrier, I say!

Breaking down the definition of policy

Let's now look at what we mean by **change, people and things** to give you a deeper feeling and understanding of the purpose of policy. This chapter is not just about definitions; it's also about bringing the definitions to life through people's lived experiences of policy examples and scenarios.

Change
Governments and organisations commit to and create **change** by influencing our behaviours, and therefore our environments, through policies.

What the heck does policy mean?

There are three components of change — inputs, outputs and outcomes. Inputs are needed to create outputs. For example, in professional sport, the inputs are the sport's overarching administrator, the individual sporting clubs and their boards, the staff (including the coach, administrative staff, medical and allied health staff), training and administrative facilities and, depending on the sport, eyewatering budgets.

Outputs are what we need to do to achieve the benefit of an outcome. The outputs (the things that the inputs do) include choosing the team's line-up and bench, training, healthy eating and team building (I'm sure there's more — you get the gist). All of these outputs are done to achieve the desired outcome: to win the final (or at least to not limp away with the wooden spoon).

To illustrate outcomes, below is an example from the Cancer Council Victoria, who in 1981 launched "Slip! Slop! Slap!" — their campaign to change Aussies' and Kiwis' attitudes and behaviours to sun protection.*

"Slip! Slop! Slap!" changed what we do when we're at the beach, in the garden, at the park with the dog, on the ski slopes — anytime we are outside. The actions of slipping on a shirt or rashie, slopping on sunscreen, and slapping on a hat are the outputs, what we need to do to not get sunburnt.[4]

Why was Cancer Council Victoria driven to do this? The high rates of, and deaths caused by, skin cancer due to repeated exposure to the sun. What did they want "Slip! Slop! Slap!" to do, i.e., what outcome did they want to achieve? To prevent sun damage to reduce the rates of skin cancer, which is an ongoing battle in this 'sunburnt country'.[5]

*Examples of real policies are presented throughout Rollercoaster. If you want to know more about a policy or how a policy played out, please do some research. Research is one of our core skills powered by our curiosity.

People and things

Public policies, at their heart, are about **people**. They are crafted to apply to a population (nationally, at a state and territory level or to a local/regional area) or to an identified group within a population. Public policies have personal and private impacts such as parental leave, available funding and support for people with autism, whom we can marry, and the age at which kids can be held criminally responsible. With just those four public policy examples, it becomes apparent that not all public policies are for all people.

Public policies can also impact people who aren't Australian citizens, such as international students, asylum seekers or short-term workers from the Pacific Islands. Further, public policies impact our relationships with and the decision-making of other nations and international organisations and companies, such as through our:

- foreign affairs policies, for example, negotiations for the reversal of prison sentences and conditions, including death penalties, for Australians convicted of a crime overseas
- trade policies, for example, getting better deals for Australian wines on international markets
- foreign investment policies, such as foreign investment in Australia's property market.

One example of a targeted public policy is the response to the closure of Australia's last car manufacturing plant that brought an end to the industry in 2017. On the heels of Ford, Toyota and General Motors closures that had started in 2013, an estimated total of 40,000–50,000 jobs ceased in Australia. Added to the personal burden and trauma of redundancy, there was nowhere for those who had lost their jobs to find the same type of work.[6]

What the heck does policy mean?

The Australian, South Australian and Victorian governments in partnership with the car manufacturers developed policies for which the key outcome was to quickly return workers retrenched from the car manufacturing industry to the labour force and included:

- supporting displaced workers to secure new work
- reducing the knock-on effects from the closures to supply chains and regional economies
- worker assistance and re-skilling programs
- creating jobs.[7]

Public policy can, however, create and perpetuate inequities. The structural inequities of Australia's superannuation system, as one example, generate disadvantages for different demographics including women, low-income earners, and Aboriginal and Torres Strait Islander people. Australia's Superannuation Guarantee was introduced in 1992 by the former Keating Government. At that time, life expectancy for Aboriginal and Torres Strait Islander people at birth was up to 20 years less than non-Indigenous Australians.[8] While the life expectancy rates for Aboriginal and Torres Strait Islander people have improved, the inequities remain. Aboriginal and Torres Strait Islander people are less likely to reach the superannuation preservation age, which means they are unable to access or spend their retirement savings.[9]

Let's now think about **things**. Policies influence just about everything connected to humans and the planet, including legal entities such as companies and businesses, the climate, the natural and built environments, flora and fauna, medicines and food, to name a few. In its space roadmap vision, Australia articulates its policy to, in part, "… build, operate and maintain off-world infrastructure and assets to expand, support and sustain humanity on Earth and in space",[10] in a mind-blowing example of people and things.

Policy development

*Genuinely listening to and considering people's feedback about our policy work are absolute musts — and our policy advice and policy development are all the better for doing these.

My dear friend, Dr Elizabeth Ganter, who has been one of the fact checkers for *Rollercoaster*, called out my use of the term policy development. *What is that?!* she cried. Actually, she called bullshit. Elizabeth didn't say I couldn't use 'policy development', though she did say, rather emphatically, that I had to explain what it is. And she's right.*

It's important to differentiate between policy makers and those who develop policy on behalf of the policy makers. A handful of times in my career, I have been asked why I chose to make certain policies. I didn't catch on at first, and then it became clear that some people thought it was my job to determine which policies should be developed and what should be in them. If only...

Here's the line of demarcation. Policy makers are those to whom I refer as the (policy) authorising environment or the (policy) decision makers throughout *Rollercoaster*. They are the people with the authority to determine the policy agenda of a government or an organisation (we'll look at this further in chapters 4 and 5). On the other hand, policy officers have two broad functions. First, policy officers provide policy makers with flat and factual (aka frank and fearless, truth to power) policy advice. Second, policy officers develop policy, including policy development recommendations they may have initiated with the authorising environment, in accordance with the policy makers' decisions and directions, and with input from an array of stakeholders.

Policy officers are on the ground with their fingers on the pulse, which provides them with valuable information, insights and understandings. However, it's the policy makers who will determine whether policy officers' evidence-informed recommendations take flight or not.

Policy development includes a myriad of functions — creating new and amending existing policy with key stakeholders, rescinding policy, monitoring and reviewing policy (it's best practice to leave evaluation to an external third party), and many things in between.

So, dear reader, policy development is what policy officers do — we develop evidence-informed policies* with input from our stakeholders, following the instruction of our authorising environment to do so. Though let me be clear: policy is nothing like a mundane cycle of rinse and repeat. Policy development is like a rollercoaster, a wrestle with gravity that leaves you feeling disoriented, dishevelled, discombobulated — and wanting more.

Takeaways

- Policy is a change.
- The changes policies create are behavioural changes.
- There are three components of a policy — the *now* is the starting point, the *what good looks like* is the end point, and the *change* happens between the two.
- While the term policy is used by governments and organisations, public policy identifies a government policy, though 'public' won't necessarily be in the title.
- On its own, the word policy is often used to refer to either public policy or policy.
- Policy officers aren't the policy makers. Policy makers are the decision makers, the authorising environment — be that the government of the day, departments' executive, or leaders of organisations outside of government.
- The job of policy officers is to provide policy makers with flat and factual policy advice, and to develop evidence-informed policy with stakeholders, including policy they may

*Evidence-based and evidence-informed are frequently used interchangeably, however, there is a difference between the two. Evidence-based refers to the explicit use of the best evidence to make decisions. Evidence-informed, while using the best evidence, also includes professional judgement and expertise including lived experience, context and values. Evidence-informed policy practice is what *bloody good* policy officers do.

have recommended, in accordance with the policy makers' decisions and directions.

Action steps

- Start to identify the following policies in your life:
  - policies that influence your work environment, such as work health and safety including psychosocial wellbeing, leave options for Australian Army reservists, or flexible working arrangements
  - policies that influence your home, for example, all the paperwork you needed to complete to rent your first home away from home
  - policies that influence your personal life, such as the extra car insurance your folks needed so that you could borrow it when you got your P-plates (I bet your parents put in some of their own policies too!)
  - policies that impact friends and family at different stages of their life, such as whether your nieces and nephews are going to be homeschooled, if your best friend can get married at the beach, and if there are public rehabilitation services close to home to help your brother get back on his feet following a mustering accident.
- Try to identify any part of your life that is *not* influenced directly or indirectly by policy. Please let me know if you think of one!

Chapter 2

Don't pass go without getting ready for implementation and evaluation

In chapter 1, we defined policy. We also noted that regardless of whether a policy is a public policy or not, policies must be definable, valuable, measurable and implementable – and this is what we are going to look at in chapter 2. We will also look at evaluation, which is only possible when a policy has been well defined, its value has been articulated, and it is measurable.

Definable

It's important to define a policy clearly, simply and succinctly for people to understand:

- why a policy is needed
- what change(s) a policy will achieve
- who will be impacted by a policy
- how we will know if a policy has been successful.

Easier said than done, trust me! It really is quite tricky to craft a policy definition that is going to be easy to understand and not pages long. While I noted in chapter 1 that the Competition Manipulation and Sport Wagering Policy[1] was a deadpan title, I have to give credit where credit is due: the title gets straight to the point, and getting straight to the point of a policy can be hard.

There's a lovely saying — *I would have written a shorter letter if I'd had more time*. No one is certain anymore as to who said it first, but it's been attributed to Blaise Pascal, Mark Twain and John Locke, to name a few. In any case, whoever penned it speaks directly to my policy heart that knows too well the highs and lows of nailing a policy definition, let alone an entire policy. There have been tears at times and imaginary wastepaper baskets overflowing with rejected drafts. However, determination, focus, grit and coffee get us through.

Start to pay attention to how different people talk about particular policies. Interviews with politicians provide great insights into how policy definitions are crafted and used to promote or, for someone opposing a policy, to completely destroy it. There is something to be said for the parallels between policy and marketing. While I'm not going to delve into marketing, governments and organisations need to 'sell' their policies; they require the 'buy-in' for their policies from their citizens, customers, clients or shareholders to get their policies over the line.

Valuable

Value, notably public value, is the combined inputs, benefits and outcomes of a public policy to the public. Public policy value is a collective one, created for and consumed by the public. Even if you're not developing public policy, you still need to identify what the value of a policy will be for your customers, clients, shareholders or volunteers.

A key reference for public servants when determining the value of a public policy and how to measure it is Mark Moore's Strategic Triangle.[2] The Strategic Triangle showed me a whole new way of thinking about and approaching policy development. If there were Strategic Triangle badges and t-shirts, I'd wear them.

What the heck does policy mean?

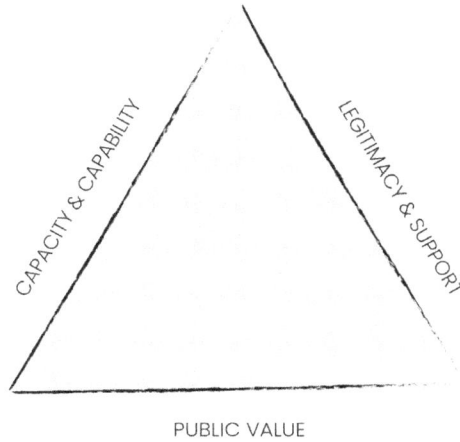

CAPACITY & CAPABILITY

LEGITIMACY & SUPPORT

PUBLIC VALUE

The Strategic Triangle presents three critical thresholds:

1. Legitimacy and support — does the government have the authority to implement a policy, and use public money to do so?
2. Capacity and capability — is there the required ability to take on additional policy work (capacity), and is there the right skill mix, ability and experience (capability) within the public service and the service providers (this could be one or a mix of public service, for-purpose and/or for-profit service providers) to develop and implement a policy?
3. Public value creation — how will a policy create public value? Read on.

The arbiters of whether a public policy has created value or not are — you guessed it! — the public. A blunt measure of whether the public has valued a government's policies is whether a government is re-elected. However, the public doesn't wait for an election to measure a policy's value. Citizens fiercely protect the policies they value, and they certainly don't rejoice when policies aren't aligned to their values.

And of course, the public isn't a homogenous collective of citizens — just think back to the conflicting values that surfaced in Australia in the lead-up to and following the Australian Indigenous Voice referendum. A policy's value will be measured by those who:

- are impacted by it and those who aren't
- support it and those who don't
- believe government should have invested elsewhere and those who believe government should have invested more into said policy
- believe the government didn't have the authority to implement the policy and by those who are angry it has taken so long
- are being regulated and those who are not.

While the above list is presented as binary options, there are many different degrees of how the public will measure a policy's value. Let's use a made-up, albeit informed, public housing policy scenario for low-income families in order to illustrate how values can differ.

The purpose of our policy scenario is to reduce the waiting times for low-income families so they can more quickly access a house. In Australia, average waiting times for public housing is anywhere from three months to five years or more. Waiting times are impacted by several variables, including:

- the availability of public housing stock
- the priority to house people with the greatest need, such as those who are experiencing homelessness or whose life or safety is at risk in their current accommodation.[3]

In our scenario, there are 15 people — an elderly couple with four adult children, a young family with three kids, and the elderly couple's neighbours, who are a family of four. The elderly couple, both on the Age Pension, have lived and raised their four children in their three-bedroom public house since they were married. There's just the two of them now; all the kids have moved out. They love their home and its memories. They want to stay there until they can no longer care for themselves.

The young family with three kids has been on a public house waitlist for over eight months. Both parents are unemployed. They're living in a mate's garage. They can use the kitchen and the bathroom in the house, but they're not looking forward to a second winter in the garage. Temporarily staying with friends or family falls under the category of homelessness.[4] This means the young family is on the priority waitlist, however, they've been told by the department there are many families ahead of them on the list.

The neighbours, a family of four, live in a private rental property. The parents earn over the income threshold to access public housing. They like the elderly couple next door. It makes the neighbours angry though that their rent keeps going up and that they don't qualify for any government support. Both parents will need to find additional work the next time the rent increases, which in their experience is always coupled with higher food and utility expenses; it's never just an isolated cost-of-living increase.

And then of course there is the government department responsible for housing. We won't count how many people make up the department, however, they are all under the pump to resolve the housing crisis. The only immediate levers available in our scenario are 1) to decant (public housing language to move people out of public housing) those tenants who live in a house that is now bigger than their initial needs into smaller properties or 2) to build new public housing.

How do you think value should be defined and measured in this scenario? Is the value an increase in the number of available three-bedroom public houses? Is the value a reduction in the number of people experiencing homelessness? Is the value in improved private housing affordability? Is the value in diversifying housing options for older Australians? Or is the value something completely different or a combination of values?

Defining value is a tough gig. Think about the policies any government has on the table now. Then turn your mind to the opposition (the main party in parliament not elected to govern), the independent members (those parliamentary members not representing a political party), media and of course the public. When a policy is being contested, it is often because the value is under question, even under fire. Despite this or perhaps because of this, capturing the value of a policy's outcome(s) is key.

Measurable and evaluation

When a policy is clearly and succinctly defined, its value can be articulated. When a policy's value is articulated, it is well positioned to be measured. When a policy can be measured, it can be evaluated. When a policy is evaluated, it can be identified whether it is driving the expected changes, for example, is the policy:

- on track to achieving *what good looks like*?
- creating unexpected positive and/or negative consequences, or having little or no impact?
- needing to be changed, completely overhauled or even rescinded?
- driving the required change(s) within expected timeframes and within budget?
- accessible, equitable?

- creating or perpetuating disadvantage?
- accepted or resisted by the public?
- accepted or resisted by those responsible for implementing it?
- accepted or resisted by those who will and won't be impacted by it?

Before we can evaluate whether a policy is working, its inputs, outputs and outcomes must all be definable and measurable. To illustrate the complexity of all the moving parts that must be defined, measured and evaluated, let's look at a real-life policy that I have simplified for the sake of example.

Annually in Australia, approximately 1,200 people are killed and a further 40,000 seriously injured on our roads.[5] Road safety strategies are focused on achieving the outcome of zero deaths and serious injuries. To achieve the outcome, all Australian governments are investing in inputs, for example, staff and resources to identify ways to reduce death and serious injuries. Input investments are expected to achieve outputs such as identified road black spots (locations where there have been a high number of accidents), improved safety features in cars, speed and traffic light cameras, reduced speed limits and the promotion of safe driving, for example, the NSW Government's 'Say *Yeah… NAH* to taking risks' campaign.[6]

The obvious measure is by how much and how quickly the road death and serious injury tolls are reducing from their quantitative baselines — 1,200 deaths and 40,000 seriously injured. Other quantitative measures could be the number of issued traffic infringements compared to previous years or the number of reduced black spots. There would also be qualitative measures — impacts to families and communities following the loss of life from avoidable accidents, impacts to individuals living with lifelong consequences of serious injuries, reduced trauma on first responders, people feeling safer on the road.

Knowing what to measure and how is a key part of evaluation. But lest you think evaluation is a final step in the process, think again: evaluations should be conducted before, during or after a policy is implemented, so we must prepare for evaluation from the start of each policy development. Put another way, develop your policy with evaluation front-of-mind.

I once joined a department right before their 10-year strategy was due for an evaluation. It became clear, as we prepared to release a tender for a third-party evaluator, that the strategy had not been structured in a way that was measurable. The *now* of when the strategy was launched was understood at a high level, as was its ultimate outcome — *we have this really big problem, and it's critical to reverse the consequences of the problem*. However, getting from the *now* (the really big problem) to *what good looks like* (reducing the drivers of the problem) was not articulated in a manner that could be measured.

This put the evaluators and the department on the back foot. It was difficult to identify exactly what changes, including the outcome, could be attributed to the strategy. We couldn't confidently credit the strategy as being successful, partially successful (on par with 'being a little bit pregnant'), on track to being successful — or having made no dent in the problem at all.

As a result, the evaluation took longer to complete, and by consequence, it was more expensive as suitable measures of inputs and outputs had to be retrofitted. It was clunky. The government of the day was not happy. The minister was not happy. The people who implemented the strategy didn't have enough evidence to demonstrate whether their hard work had driven the desired change. And the people who were impacted by the strategy, while they had their own lived experience, were left in the dark as to whether they were going to benefit from the long-term difference they had been promised.

Ten years is a big investment and a long commitment. Acknowledging that this strategic policy was developed at a time when approaches were different, it does emphasise that it is crucial to have robust, flat and factual evidence to demonstrate whether a policy investment was worth it or not.

Implementable

Implementation is an evidence-informed process of translating a policy into practice, action and behavioural change. There are two immediate takeaways from the definition of implementation. One, evidence, policy and implementation must be linked. Two, we must prepare as much for policy implementation as we do for policy development; we don't leave either to chance.

There are three phases of implementation:

1. Pre-implementation — the time required to prepare for implementation
2. Implementation — the number or proportion of activities completed
3. Sustainability — how far implementation has progressed.[7]

There are three significant risks if we leave implementation to chance:

- The operational teams and service providers are unable to translate the policy into their service delivery model.

- The behavioural changes the policy is trying to influence can't be achieved by either or both the operational teams and service providers and those who will be impacted by a policy.
- A policy's inputs, outputs and outcomes won't be measurable to identify if a policy is driving its desired change(s).

To control these risks and to increase the probability of getting policy right, we must engage the above three groups of people from the moment we commence policy development. Let's look at why they are important.

Operational and service teams and providers expected to deliver a policy understand and can provide implementation context and reality to:

- the capacity and capability of their staff and leaders to embed a new policy into their service delivery model
- the environmental suitability and readiness for a policy
- the willingness of and acceptance of a policy by the intended recipients/beneficiaries
- suitable systems for and monitoring methods of implementation and outcomes, and whether these systems are readily available and accessible.

People with lived experience and those who will be impacted by a policy provide implementation context and reality about:

- whether their agency is respected and recognised or whether their agency is being diminished or removed
- their willingness and acceptance to change their behaviours as required by a policy
- their acceptance of the proposed public value

- personal impact and cost.

Review, monitoring and evaluation experts provide policy and implementation context and reality about:

- how to best structure a policy so that it can be reviewed, monitored and evaluated
- existing secondary research and statistical analyses that apply to a policy
- where a policy may require primary research, i.e., there are no reputable or relevant secondary research sources that can be used and therefore, a specific research capacity needs to be established
- the type of evaluation relevant to a policy and the timeframes required to measure from, for example, real-time evaluation to longitudinal studies.

We know policy is a change. When a policy pivots to implementation, the change becomes real. The change can even become a disruption. Change, including a change that is desired, can be challenging. Disruption is often less welcome. We need to anticipate different responses to change and disruption, and how they will impact each policy's implementation and implementation sustainability.

Key questions we need to ask ourselves — the operational and service teams and providers; people with lived experience and those who will be impacted by a policy; and review, monitoring and evaluation experts — are:

- What needs to be done?
- How should 'it' be done and by whom?
- Is 'it' desirable?
- Can 'it' be done?

- Can 'it' be done within available funding and resources?
- Can we do 'it'?
- Can they do 'it'?
- Is there a better or different way of doing 'it'?
- How will we know 'it' has been done?

There is one last crucial learning I want to share with you about implementation. Use implementation to understand where, how, why and when a policy can fail. When you consider a policy from a failure perspective, you have a far greater opportunity to identify controls for failure early, giving policies a better chance of getting to *what good looks like*.

Takeaways

- Any policy that is not definable, valuable, measurable and implementable is *not* a policy. Call it Betty if you want, but don't call it a policy.
- From the moment a policy hits your desk, start considering implications for its implementation and evaluation.
- For every policy to have a reasonable opportunity to drive the desired change, policy officers must genuinely embrace working with other experts, including data and evaluation experts, those who will be implementing, people with lived experience and those who will be impacted.
- Take the time to consider how a policy will provide value to the public.
- Remember, there will be many different expectations and understandings of a policy's value.
- Policies must create value, and the public are the arbiters of public value creation.

Action steps

- Actively listen to:
  - how politicians promote or comprehensively annihilate policies
  - what influencers — the business community, former politicians, community leaders — are saying about a policy
  - what policy questions the media is asking
  - what the people in your life — colleagues, friends, family — think and say about policies.
- Start to consider how you measure the value of a public policy that directly impacts you.
- Read everything you can lay your hands on about the Strategic Triangle.
- Each time a policy task hits your desk, see if the Strategic Triangle's three questions can be answered. If they can't, check in with your supervisor.
- If you're not hearing the words 'measuring', 'implementation' or 'evaluation' in discussions you're involved with — take a big breath of courage (if you need it) and start asking some simple questions:
  - How can this be measured?
  - Do we know who will be implementing the policy? How do we get them involved early?
  - What organisations could we engage to understand the needs and concerns of the people who will be impacted by the policy?
  - What would be expected for an external evaluator to look at in two, five, ten years' time?
- Make your own implementation list. Add questions to the list on pp. 29-30 or start a brand new one. The more you are

actively thinking about implementation (and everything else in this chapter), the more comfortable you will feel discussing, exploring and advising on these key policy elements.

Chapter 3

The policy smorgasbord

There are four groups of policies — public policies, strategic polices, departmental and operational policies. Rest assured the definition of policy holds regardless of the type of policy it is. However, in the policy world, there are two other big players — legislation and regulation. It's also important to understand the inter- and intra-dependencies between legislation, regulation and policy, and we'll return to this in chapter 7.

Here's what we're going to do in this chapter. First, we'll have a quick look at what legislation and regulation are. Second, we'll get stuck into the smorgasbord of the different policy types, and third, we'll briefly consider what can trigger a policy.

A sneak peek at legislation and regulation

Legislation are the laws made by a parliament — federal, state or territory. In Australia, only parliaments can make laws. Laws create structures that regulate and influence the way people, organisations and governments are to behave. Sound familiar? Yep, legislation has the same underpinning definition as policy. Peas in a pod, though definitely not identical twin peas! Note that the words legislation and law(s) are used interchangeably, including in *Rollercoaster*.

Regulation is the administration of any law or rule that is put in place by a government. By default, a regulation includes compliance —

there are established expectations about who is required to comply with a law or rule and what that compliance looks like — i.e., what people are expected to do and not do. Regulations are delegated laws (sometimes referred to as subordinate legislation), meaning a parliament has given a minister, a department, an agency or others the authority to administer a law or rule.

Regulations are:

*Unlike titles of legislation, titles of regulation are not italicised.

**The abbreviation in brackets, for example (Qld) or (Cth), in the title of a law indicates the jurisdiction of the parliament that has passed the legislation. The year highlighted in an act's title is the year the first time the law was assented in a parliament. Dates of following amendments are identified in versions that supersede previous versions, though the year the first time the law was assented in a parliament remains.

- Intentional — they are focused on a specific law and its requirements, for example, the Child Protection Regulation 2023 (Qld)* provides for administrative decision making and operational processes under (and only under) the *Child Protection Act 1999* (Qld).**
- Monitored and enforced — regulatory bodies derive their functions and powers from an act of parliament to monitor and enforce specific pieces of legislation. For example, under the *Reserve Bank Act 1959* (Cth), the Reserve Bank of Australia is responsible for, among other things, regulating Australia's monetary policy and for the issuing of Australia's currency.
- Purposeful — they have specific goals to attain and maintain. The Aboriginal Areas Protection Authority, for example, is the regulator for the protection of Aboriginal sacred sites in the NT.

Many authorities in Australia are responsible for administering and enforcing regulation. More than 500 local governments (aka local councils) regulate, among other things, how we should manage our dogs, cats, chooks and llamas, who can get a film permit and whether you can hold a fundraising event at the botanical gardens. Park authorities regulate the conservation and enhancement of national parks. State and territory education departments regulate schools, including making sure parents and guardians enrol their kids and that their kids turn up every day. The Therapeutic Goods Administration regulates how medicines are manufactured and certified. And you know what — regulations need policies. Why? Because not only departments but also organisations outside of government will need their own internal policies to make sure they are compliant with regulations.

We will look further into legislation and regulation in chapter 7. In the interim, consider the below illustration that neatly captures what is commonly referred to as the policy hierarchy and which stands true for public policy and for policy outside of government. Notice how legislation sits at the top and how it needs a whole lot of help from policy to hold on to its hierarchical alpha position. Just saying.

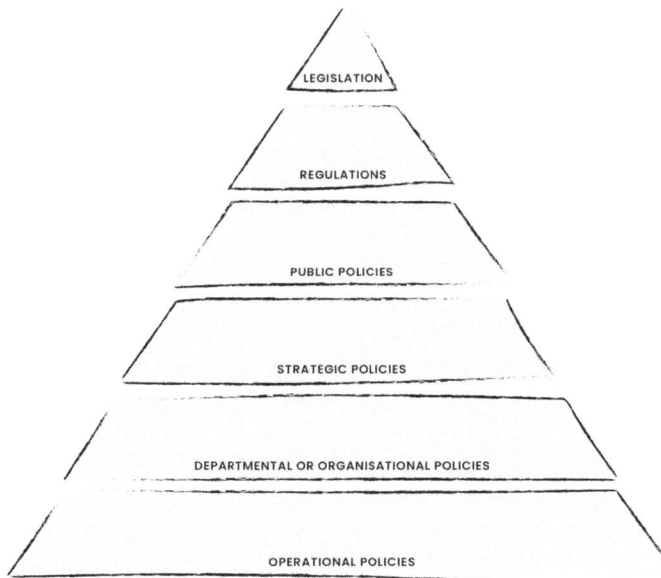

The different policy types

Public policy

We know from chapter 1 that public policy is a government policy commitment for the people and is often used when referring broadly to public policies, for example, public health policies, public infrastructure policies or public fiscal policies. We also know that the word 'public' is often not used. However, we must remember that public policy is the currency of governments and their public services.

I sense you might be thinking that government and public services' currency would be the economy. A key focus of any government is indeed building the economy. However, no matter what or how a government or public service does, it is underpinned by policy. Every. Single. Time.

There is more than one type of policy though — there's a whole suite of the stuff, as illustrated in the policy hierarchy on p. 35, and which we are about to explore. (The same policy types are also relevant to organisations outside of government.) Each policy definition, relevant to a public service, will include:

- the policy type name
- other names that the policy type is also known as — these aren't exhaustive lists; you're bound to learn more, and I'd wager new names will be coined over the course of your career
- defining features
- how the policy type is aligned to the definition of policy
- examples of the same policy type from organisations outside of government or a public service.

Leaving legislation and regulation aside for the moment, let's explore each of the policy types in the pyramid more closely.

Strategic policy

Other names: strategic plan, framework, development strategy, investment strategy, roadmap.

Strategic policy defining features

- an intentional shift from a government policy commitment to a department policy responsibility
- a public and an internal statement of a department's vision, purpose and values. Note there are differences in the wording from department to department. For example, some strategic policies will flag principles, outcomes or 'why this is important'
- distinct commitments that signpost how a department will contribute to a government's policy agenda plus how a department will commit to its own strategic objectives, such as workforce development
- articulated high-level goals and how those goals are to be achieved. For example, SA's Attorney-General's Department Strategic Plan has six goals, each supported by priority actions[1]
- a defined date range or target date, for example, the Strategic Plan 2023–27, Department of the Premier and Cabinet, Queensland,[2] and the WA Department of Energy, Mines, Industry Regulation and Safety, Towards 2029[3]
- rely on and can amend or trigger the need for new departmental and operational policies and guidelines.

It's becoming more common to see strategic policies presented on one to two pages (very different to what once was the standard of very long strategic policies — both in the number of pages and in their defined date range), further illustrating how they provide a high-level overview of a department's strategic policy intentions, such as Victoria's Planning on a Page (which is actually two pages, but who's counting?).[4]

Additional to a department's overarching strategic policy, departments will often have a strategic policy for each key responsibility, for example, the 24-Hour Economy Strategy of NSW's Department of Creative Industries, Tourism, Hospitality and Sport.[5]

Strategic policy definition alignment

A strategic policy's date range or target date indicates the length of time it will be active. The starting date captures the *now*, and the end date indicates when *what good looks like* is anticipated to be achieved. The content of a strategic policy — key priority areas and priority actions — identifies at a high level what and how desired changes will be achieved within the given timeframe.

Examples of strategic policies outside government or a public service:

- Foodbank's National Food Security Strategy[6]
- Strategic Plan Bowls NT 2024[7]
- AusCycling United Strategy 2032.[8]

Departmental policy

Other names: departmental policy is a catch-all for the policies that structure and inform how departments will achieve their strategic policy(ies), and include (though definitely not limited to):

- division, business unit and team business plans
- work health and safety policies
- human resource policies
- optional uniform policy
- code of conduct
- financial delegations
- positive duty policy.

Departmental policies are often required by legislation, for example, work health and safety and positive duty policies. Others may not be required by law, for example, an optional uniform policy — though they, as with all policies, must be lawful.

Departmental policy defining features

Departmental policies provide more detail than strategic policies. They stipulate behaviours, articulate expectations, and clarify boundaries and protocols as to 'how we do business here'. Departmental policies establish a department's operating environment's culture, norms and practices.

Some, though not all, departmental policies will be public-facing documents, such as the South Australian Heritage Council's complaints policy.[9]

Departmental policy definition alignment

Departmental policies anchor and frame staff — and sometimes also the public's — behaviours from the *now*, that is, the point in time when a specific requirement is needed. For example, a staff member required to travel for work will need to follow their department's staff travel policy and seek approval as per their department's financial delegations. The *what good looks like* is the individual and collective effort to execute their responsibilities in accordance with department protocols, processes, obligations, transparency and accountability.

Examples of organisational (intentional name change from departmental) policies outside of government or a public sector:

- Coogee Beach Surf Life Saving Club, Club Honours Policy[10]
- Airbnb, Cancellation policies for your listing[11]
- Floriade Terms & Conditions[12] (note the different language!).

Operational policy

Other names: procedures, standard operating procedures, processes, practice code, standing orders, standards, and duties. Remember in chapter 1 when I noted that other departments or organisations may have more or different policy definitions than yours — this is exactly what I mean!

Operational policy defining features

While operational policy can be part of departmental policy, I put it into its own basket as it explicitly details how a role, function, task or procedure must be carried out or delivered. Operational policies are often collated into manuals so that staff follow the same processes each time.

Some department's operational policies will be public-facing, though they are more than likely to have a title that reflects the subject of the policy — such as the Department of Foreign Affairs and Trade's (DFAT) 'Passports'[13] — than a title that includes 'operational policy'. DFAT's Passports is also an example of an operational policy that not only outlines what is required of the department but also includes requirements of everyday folks who need a passport.

Guidelines can also fall under this policy type, with the fundamental difference being that there is often greater room for discretion in guidelines than in operational policy. Police officers, for example, have discretion in how they deal with alleged minor drug offences by deciding whether to divert adults (and, in some jurisdictions, young people) to drug diversion programs or to charge them. However, a government public policy focus such as zero tolerance or blitzes on criminal behaviour will absolutely influence, if not suspend, police officers' discretion, and in this example, require police to strictly follow operational procedure.

Operational policy definition alignment

By nature, operational policies embody the definition of policy. Operational policies require staff to behave and conduct their duties in a specific way to achieve the same desired change every time. Consider the passport example of an operational policy. The *now* for DFAT is to ensure a secure, efficient and responsive passport service. The *now* for the passport applicants its being able to get their passport in time to meet their travel requirements. The *what good looks like* for DFAT is achieving key performance indicators that demonstrate they are providing a secure, efficient and responsive passport service, and for applicants, it's being able to hop on that plane or cruise for the trip of a lifetime. The passport policy is the vehicle of change that makes *what good looks like* happen.

Please remember, however, that while I have included guidelines under operational policy, guidelines differ in that they provide for discretion.

Examples of operational policies outside of government or a public sector:

- MONA's privacy policy[14]
- Crown Perth's terms of entry[15]
- MCG's emergency evacuation procedure.[16]

When things can get a bit blurry

Sometimes it's hard to neatly pop policies into specific boxes and work out what type of policy they are and how they are directly related, or not, to other policies, legislation and regulation. To start to get a feel for this, let's look at four policy examples — a public policy commitment, a return policy, a dress code and an appropriate behaviours policy.

From commitment to action

Policy commitments are part of governments' (and wannabe governments') day-to- day routine. Food for thought — the Australian Constitution (which we'll look at in chapter 4) does not recognise election commitments. The Constitution only recognises commitments made by an elected government. However, many a government does hold true to its commitments, which become strategic policies. Though it doesn't stop there. Strategic policies will rely on other policies, including departmental policies, at times legislation and regulation, and they will need operational policies to take them from written statements to reality.

By default, policy development is not a quick process, sometimes taking years to get off the ground. However, there are exceptions — governments' responses to Covid-19 being an obvious and extreme example. Let's take a look at how some of it played out from a policy development perspective.

What the heck does policy mean?

Governments' actions to protect their nations took many forms, like the availability of vaccines and mandated vaccination requirements. In rapid succession, a public policy commitment became a strategic policy that drove and relied on multiple changes to introduce and activate the following (among many more):

- legislation and regulations
- departmental policies across public sectors, for instance —
  - Staff were moved from what were considered non-priority areas to support essential services, the procurement and distribution of medical supplies, and the rostering and placement of medical and medical support staff.
  - Cross-departmental policy staff were combined to produce new policies that required regular updates in accordance with the impacts of and changing government responses, including legislative and regulatory responses, to the pandemic.
  - Staff numbers were limited at the workplace and working from home policies were introduced to reduce the risk of the spread of Covid-19 and hopefully maintain the capacity of public services to serve their communities.
- adjustment to existing and introduction of new operational policies, for example —
  - police, military and bio-security staff conducting quarantine and lockdown compliance checks
  - travel restrictions and international border controls
  - provision of remote and flexible learning for school students
  - provision of repurposed aged care sites to provide people experiencing homelessness a place to self-isolate.

Let's now look at our other three examples. If you're struggling to distinguish between policy versus public policy versus legislation, don't worry — you will get the hang of it after a while!

Australian Consumer Law and your favourite homeware store's return policy

By law — specifically, the *Australian Consumer Law 2010* (Cth) (ACL) — your favourite homeware store is required to have a return policy outlining what you need to do to return an item and how the store is to manage the return. At a minimum, the homeware store owner must meet ACL requirements, but this doesn't stop the owner from being more generous with their return policy. For example, they could offer a full refund for certain products if you change your mind within 48 hours of your purchase (which is not required by the ACL). No wonder you love shopping there! While the ACL is legislation founded in public policy and applies across the country, the application of it in your favourite homeware store is not in itself a public policy. The homeware store's return policy is an operational policy to meet their legal obligations and to look after their customers.

The dress code — what should I wear?

What to wear is an important consideration — if only to ensure you are not breaking the law by "wilfully and obscenely exposing your person" in public (just like those cheeky streakers at the footy and the cricket). Sometimes we don't need to frantically empty the wardrobe or scramble through the dirty wash in a vain effort to find an outfit not too crumpled or smelly to wear to work because our company may have a dress code (the uniform for which could also be lying in a smelly heap on the floor). Venues too have dress codes for how they wish their patrons, visitors and staff to be attired. It's quite likely your favourite watering hole has a dress code. Dress codes in this instance aren't a public policy; they are the venue's operational policy. Other dress codes are legislated, like the uniforms worn by the police and the military.

In yet another example, Australia's Parliament House has a dress code. While that's to be expected, you might be surprised to learn that it got them into hot water when, in 2018, Australian journalist Patricia Karvelas was asked to leave for breaching the dress code. High scandal — Karvelas had not covered her arms. Even in Australia's Parliament House, the heartland of Australian public policy, the dress code isn't a public policy. The officials' actions could have been legally challenged if they were found to be discriminatory because anti-discrimination laws, not dress codes, are founded in public policy. Remember — policies, including public policies, whether compelled by legislation or not, must be lawful.

Keeping your cool at the kids' soccer match (or whatever they play)

It's not always the kids who play up; we adults also need to be reminded from time to time to pull our heads in. Poor parental and spectator behaviour at kids sporting matches can ruin a fun family afternoon at best, and be seriously problematic or dangerous, even horrifically tragic, at worst. Play by the Rules was developed in 2001 by South Australia's Department for Sport and Recreation and has been adopted across states and territories as a valuable tool to protect children while they are playing sport.[17] Play by the Rules is a platform that educates and informs everyone involved in kids' sports, from parents to coaches and volunteers, about protecting children from a range of harms including discrimination, harassment and bullying. While not a public policy, there is a good chance that Play by the Rules underpins your kids' sport club's policy suite.

Policy triggers

A policy can be triggered at any time. Policies can be triggered during an election, during a term of government as part of regular business, in response to an unexpected emergency or to community calls for change, and as a consequence of introduced (new) or amended legislation, or even rescinded legislation.

A thousand things (and then some) can trigger a need for a policy. It might be the importance to protect Aboriginal and Torres Strait Islander peoples' traditional knowledge and cultural material.[18] It might be the impact of introduced pests, such as the Asian longhorn beetle (don't get me started on cane toads), on Australia's biodiversity.[19] It might be the limited opportunities in professional development for young dancers.[20] Or it might be niche market challenges for Australian craft beer brewers.[21]

Why am I telling you this? Because so often I hear people say that policy is just about rules and regulation. Policy can be that, but it's so much more. Policy, as I have said previously, impacts every part of our life, and therefore, the need for policy can be triggered by so many different things — which, to me, makes policy pretty darn exciting.

Takeaways

- In the hierarchy of policy, legislation is at the top of the list.
- Strategic policies lift government policies from the page to the real world and set the high-level agenda for government departments and other organisation types.
- Organisational or departmental policies describe how organisations and departments 'do' their business.

- Operational policies explicitly detail how roles, functions, tasks and procedures should be carried out or delivered; guidelines are similar, though usually with more discretion.
- Departments' and organisations' policies collectively form their policy suite.
- There is a domino effect in the policy suite — each triggering the next or relying on another policy type before coming into play.

Action steps

- When talking about policy and policy types with others, always check their definitions to make sure you are talking about the same thing — there are many definitions out there!
- The span of policy types presents many career opportunities for policy officers, particularly in government departments and large organisations. I highly recommend you actively seek opportunities to work across different policy areas. This will increase your experience, provide you with valuable insights and take you to that next policy job you're chasing.
- There are multiple policy triggers, and they don't all start at a government's cabinet table or during your policy team's meetings. Take note of what has triggered policies in your area across all policy types.

Part 2:

The system

"Chaos Theory: a delicious contradiction — a science of predicting behaviour of 'inherently unpredictable' systems... From the outside, they display unpredictable and chaotic behaviour but expose the inner workings, and you discover a perfectly deterministic set of equations ticking like clockwork".

Borwein J & Rose M 2012, Explainer: what is Chaos Theory 2012 (The Conversation)

The system

A treat awaits in Part 2 where we get a taste of chaos theory firsthand as we explore the apparent contradiction of how things work in Australia, that is, through the deterministic equation of the Australian Constitution, the Westminster System and the machinery of government (MoG).

These are big concepts; however, I have intentionally streamlined the content in *Rollercoaster*. I want to share key elements that will assist you in navigating the system you work in. It's crucial that you understand the different connected and moving parts, their purpose, and what this means for you.

In chapter 4, we will consider Australia's legal foundation — the Australian Constitution. The Constitution is the rules and rights book for Australia's authorising environment and its citizens. The Constitution establishes how powers are distributed, executed and kept in check.

In chapter 5, we'll move on to the Westminster system, which is the system of parliamentary government in Australia, and that too of other Commonwealth countries. The principle of the Westminster system is that the executive government is responsible to the people of Australia, through its parliaments. We'll also look at the mechanisms of governance that come into play across the system.

Machinery of governments, often referred to as MoGs, are the focus of chapter 6. MoGs are shaped and structured by the Australian Constitution and the Westminster system; they reflect the strategic policy priorities of the government of the day (remember, there are nine governments in Australia, which means there are nine, albeit similar, MoGs in Australia*). A MoG is how a government and its public service are structured and interconnected, and includes systems, processes, and the allocation of functions and

*The Australian Bureau of Statistics includes other territories, islands, development areas, and territorial waters and enclaves in both its geographic and economic statistics that are not included in *Rollercoaster*.

responsibilities between ministers and 'their' departments. You are part of your jurisdiction's MoG!

Are you ready? It might be time to grab a cuppa and a packet of your favourite biccies.

Chapter 4

The Australian Constitution

The Australian Constitution[1, 2]

I remember exactly where I was and who I was with when I heard for the first time that Australia had a constitution. I wish I could say I was in class with either Mrs Angus or Mr Green, my two favourite primary school teachers. Alas, I was heading back to the office after a cross-agency meeting with my then boss. Two thoughts collided in my mind. First was, *What, we have a constitution too?!* Second, *Don't say out loud what you just thought.* And when no one was looking, I checked the veracity of this seemingly crazy, unfounded statement. Needless to say, it was neither crazy nor unfounded. And no, I have never admitted to this extraordinary gap in my (adult) knowledge. And now I'm declaring it in a book. Go figure.

Since that moment of profound enlightenment, I have not become a constitutional lawyer or expert. Nothing close. However, I have made sure that I understand how the Australian Constitution influences policy development, and it's important you understand this too. Before we consider the Constitution's six principles, we'll have a quick look at how it came into play over 125 years ago.

When the *Commonwealth of Australia Constitution Act 1900* (Cth) (commonly known as the Australian Constitution) was passed by the British Parliament, the then-proclaimed six British Colonies — New South Wales, Victoria, South Australia (including the northern territory of South Australia*), Queensland, Tasmania and Western Australia (aka the reluctant state as it was the last state to vote in

*In 1863, the then Colony of South Australia acquired the NT from NSW, which it surrendered to the Commonwealth of Australia in 1907, meaning the NT was governed by the Australian Government. Seventy-one years later, *the Northern Territory (Self Government) Act 1978* (Cth) was passed. As for the Australian Capital Territory (ACT), it was surrendered by NSW to the Commonwealth of Australia in 1909 and had to wait until 1988 until the *Australian Capital Territory (Self Government) Act 1988* (Cth) was passed. While both territories have legislative powers, they do not benefit from the full legislative independence that the Australian Constitution provides the states.

favour) — were united. When the Commonwealth of Australia was declared, the united states (not to be confused, as I clearly had, with the other United States) were referred to as a federation of states, and the Federal Government was established.

When considering the Constitution, it is important to remember who and what existed at the time of its creation.* The monarch of the day was Queen Victoria, who was driven to expand the British Empire. Perhaps constitutional scholars would challenge me on this; however, I see Queen Victoria's focus to expand the British Empire as her reigning public policy.

*The language of the Australian Constitution has not changed since it was passed in 1901. The use of 'her' references Queen Victoria and extends to her heirs and successors in the sovereignty of the United Kingdom, regardless of the reigning monarch's gender (I think we're a way off from a monarch identifying as non-binary). The apparent language gap as well as the missing reference to the territories, the ACT and the NT reflect that in 1901, neither were established as self-governments.

The Constitution doesn't define the prime minister, nor does it define (the) cabinet, let alone all cabinets of Australia. Nor, as mentioned above, does it consider the ACT or the NT. While the Constitution talks to the rights of Australians, I would argue that it was written to exclude certain Australians.

The passing of the *Commonwealth of Australia Constitution Act 1900* and the declaration of Australia as terra nullius, a land belonging to no one, dispossessed Aboriginal and Torres Strait Islander people of their lands, the core of their spirituality, and stripped them of community identities, shattered kinships, broke community and language groups, and ignored customs and law. The trauma and consequences of these losses reverberate across Australia to this day.

Ninety-one years later, the High Court of Australia overturned the British Parliament's declaration of Australia as terra nullius, finding the declaration to be legal fiction — an assumption that purports to or does conceal, alter, or modify a fact or rule of the law.[3]

The Constitution is a document of its time, and while it has been amended eight times since it took effect, it still clashes with who and what Australia is today — or tries to be from time to time.

If like me, you are a non-Indigenous person, I believe we have a responsibility as policy officers to take particular care when developing policies that will impact First Nations people. At a minimum, we must always seek their guidance, counsel and direction and develop these policies with them. They've had a crippling amount of policy 'done to them'.

The Australian Constitution's six principles[4]

To know how the Australian Constitution works is to understand its six principles — democracy, the rule of law, the separation of powers, federalism, nationhood and rights. I think it's also fair to add that a true understanding of the Constitution means recognising who and what it is silent about.

Democracy

The foundation of Australia's democracy is that its citizens elect their parliamentary representatives — in fact, voting is mandatory for all Australians.* Elections occur frequently at the federal, state, territory and local government levels. Australian Government elections are held every three years, and state, territory and local government elections are held every four years. There are also by-elections which take place when a seat, or seats, becomes vacant in any government. This results in all Australian jurisdictions having an elected parliament and a system of representative government (the party or coalition that wins the vote).

*Not all nations in the Commonwealth have mandatory voting, and not all election cycles of the 56 Commonwealth countries are the same. For example, like the Australian Government, New Zealand has a prescribed three-year term; however, Gabon a seven-year term; Kiribatis a four-year term; and Singapore, Saint Lucia and Cyprus five-year terms.

There is a hierarchy of government, with the Australian Government at the top. Keep this in mind as you develop policies, as the Australian Government may have a policy, indeed legislation and regulations, that can relate to and influence your work. Let's have a quick look at the government hierarchy and structure.

Australian government hierarchy

The Federal Government, as established by the Constitution, now goes by multiple names that are used interchangeably — the Federal Government, the Commonwealth Government and the Australian Government. Sometimes you might hear a blend of naming conventions, for example, the Australian Federal Government. At other times, usually in informal settings or when a state or territory wishes to make a rather firm point, the Australian Government is simply called 'Canberra'! Why? Because the city of Canberra is the seat of the Australian Parliament.* In *Rollercoaster*, I use the terms Australian Government and Australian Parliament unless I am referencing a naming convention or a direct quote.

Today, Australia has three tiers of government — the Australian Government, the six states and two territories, and local government. Each tier of government is physically represented (that is, there are departments, agencies and public servants) in each jurisdiction, noting there is no separate local government in the the ACT**, nor is there an Australian local government.

Rule of law

The rule of law is the principle that everyone, regardless of status and including all organisations and tiers of government, is answerable to the same laws. The rule of law explicitly articulates and restricts powers. For example, the Constitution defines what parliaments can do, such

*Next time you hear an ad from a government, keep your ear out for what is said at the end, which is usually something like ... *authorised by [name], Canberra*. States and territories use the same statement (obviously namedropping where their own seat of parliament is) in their advertising. The purpose of saying this is to identify where the authority for the ad comes from.

**The ACT Assembly is different to that of other jurisdictions in that it performs territory *and* local government functions.

54

as the Australian Parliament's powers to legislate for astronomical and meteorological observation; weights and measures; and lighthouses, lightships, beacons and buoys — states and territories do not have the power to legislate in these areas. The Constitution also identifies what a parliament can't do, such as neither the Australian Parliament (nor the Australian Government) can influence or change a decision of a court, for example, the High Court's ruling that Australia's system of indefinite immigration detention is unlawful.

Just in case your head isn't spinning yet, there is a naming convention you need to be aware of too. You may have noticed that I don't refer to Australian legislation. That's because laws passed by the Australian Parliament are Commonwealth laws and are usually referenced as such in formal documents and settings (though not always on the telly).

Primacy of Commonwealth legislation

Section 109 of Australia's Constitution specifically refers to the primacy of Commonwealth legislation over state and territory legislation. This means two things:

1. If a Commonwealth law is inconsistent with a state law, the Commonwealth law prevails to the extent of the inconsistency.
2. The Commonwealth has the power to override state laws.

You can research relevant Commonwealth legislation to see if there are inconsistencies with your jurisdiction's legislation; however, it's difficult to anticipate where, why, how or when Commonwealth legislation might apply to what you are working on. When in doubt seek advice from your supervisor as to how to best approach this.

However, section 122 is an additional kicker for the territories. Under section 122, the Australian Parliament is able to enlarge or diminish the grant of self-government to any of its territories as it sees fit.[5] Earlier, I mentioned the *Northern Territory (Self Government) Act 1978* (Cth). Did you notice that it's Commonwealth legislation? Keep this keep in mind for what's coming next.

Two examples of how the Australian Parliament can diminish a grant of self-government and flex its legislative power are the overturning of the *Rights of the Terminally Ill Act 1995* (NT) and the *Northern Territory National Emergency Response Act 2007* (Cth). Let's look at these examples a bit closer as they bring to light not only the primacy of Commonwealth legislation, but also that the territories have far lesser legislative powers than their state counterparts.

In 1995, the NT became the first jurisdiction in the world to legalise euthanasia thanks to a private member's bill (being a member of the opposition or an independent member's bill). It's not unusual for a private member, as opposed to a government minister, to introduce bills to parliament. However, private members' bills are usually trickier to get passed if the government opposes them. Though the Terminally Ill bill was passed on the floor of the NT Parliament, however, it was consequently overturned by the Australian Parliament in 1997. The ban prevented not only the NT but also the ACT from passing voluntary assisted dying legislation. Twenty-five years later, the Australian Parliament overturned its ban on euthanasia laws in the ACT and the NT. In October 2023, the ACT Government introduced the Voluntary Assisted Dying Bill. Subsequent updates are outside the scope of this book, but it would be an interesting legislative story for you to follow.

In 2007, in response to the *Ampe Akelyernemane Meke Mekarle "Little Children are Sacred Report"*,[6] the Howard [Liberal] Government, with bipartisan support from the leader of the Opposition, introduced the *Northern Territory National Emergency Response Act 2007* (Cth). This act provided for the Australian Government, without requiring the NT's consent or support, "to improve the well-being of certain communities in the NT" (a total of 69 Aboriginal lands, community living areas and town camps).

The primacy of the Commonwealth legislation became highly controversial; one because the Australian Government came in over the top of the NT Government and two, it smacked of a paternalistic intervention that many had hoped was a thing of the past. Following a change of government, the 'Intervention' became the subject of a review board established by the Rudd [Labor]* Australian Government. The review board found that the Intervention was a "collective imposition based on race... and that the positive potential measures [were] dampened and delayed by the manner in which they were imposed".[7] Following four separate amendments to this act, it was repealed in July 2012 by the Gillard [Labor] Government.

However, in some instances, states and territories do have concurrent powers with the Commonwealth to legislate matters that are not specifically listed in the Constitution. Read on.

Commonwealth, state and territory concurrent powers to make laws

There are Commonwealth, state and territory laws for what appears to be the same matter — though there are notable differences. Let's look at the *Australian Education Act 2013* (Cth) as an example.

The *Australian Education Act 2013* (Cth) legislates how the Australian Government funds government and non-government schools across

*In 1908, it was the Australian *Labour* Party, though in 1912 the party changed the spelling to *Labor*. This might come in handy at an upcoming quiz night.

Australia to "ensure that the Australian schooling system provides a high quality and highly equitable education for all students". Don't skim this bit: the act also requires schools to implement national policy initiatives and education reforms as well as comply with extensive funding requirements.

At the same time, education legislation at the state and territory levels establishes broader requirements of how schools are administered, staffed and operated; the compulsory school age; the delivery of home education; and so much more. If you're counting, that makes nine (total Commonwealth, state and territories) pieces of education legislation with two different purposes, and one being exclusive to Commonwealth legislative powers.

Separation of powers

The Constitution divides powers between three separate bodies — the legislature, the executive government and the judiciary — aka, the parliament, the government and the courts. The same distribution of powers is reflected in each state and territory's constitution.

The purposes of the separation of powers are to:

- provide checks and balances
- ensure that one power cannot override another
- ensure that not all powers are vested in one body that could abuse its powers (as so aptly illustrated in Marvel© comics).

Each body can only execute the distinct powers it has been given (for instance, the judicature can't legislate), as follows:

- Parliaments have the power to make laws (legislative power).
- Executive governments have the powers to administer laws and carry out the business of government (administrative powers).

- The judicature has the power to determine legal disputes (judicial power).*

We'll come back to the separation of powers in chapter 5; for now, let's move on to federalism.

Federalism

We've already touched on federalism in this chapter. Scroll up, turn back a couple of pages or rewind the audio to the Australian government hierarchy and the rule of law if you need a refresher. There are, however, a couple of other things to point out regarding federalism, namely:

- Federal powers have grown since federation, reflecting how our society has changed and evolved (in some areas) since 1901. However, the Australian Parliament's powers are still conferred, meaning it can't act in areas outside of its powers.
- Federalism ensures that states maintain a continued independence; the Australian Government cannot place burdens that would affect their ability to function. However, and as we considered under the primacy of Commonwealth legislation and the Australian Parliament's ability to enlarge or diminish the grant of self-government to any of its territories as it sees fit, the territories are exposed to what some might see as much needed assistance from, and others might see as interference by, the Australian Government.
- Differences between governments and their citizens are played out daily on the political stage. However, if there is difference that raises constitutional issues, the High Court will step in to resolve it.

*Judges certainly have the time to consider many a legal dispute. In Australia, judges have tenure 'forever' or until they turn 72 — that's an extraordinary commitment.

Nationhood

Though it is one of the Constitution's six principles, we are not going to dwell on nationhood here. What is important to point out now is that nationhood is defined by a nation's system of government, and we're going to look at this in the next chapter.

Rights

The Constitution doesn't have a long list of rights — in fact, it's surprisingly short. The rights cover:

- religious freedoms, though limitations are imposed on the way we manifest a religion or belief
- acquisition of property by the Commonwealth, however, states do not have to comply, which may not be as straightforward for the territories, if the Commonwealth so chooses
- challenging the actions of governments and their ministers if found to be unlawful
- trial by jury for Australian citizens for serious Commonwealth offences, though some trials in state courts do not have juries
- the right of a resident of one state to move freely between states and to not be treated less favourably than the residents of another state
- free trade and commerce among the states.

There are also two implied rights:

- the right to vote, though not for all prisoners
- the right to political communication.

The interest of a short list was underpinned in the belief that our democratic process would protect our rights. Regardless of the length of the list, it is critical that rights, as with all the Constitution's principals, are fully respected and reflected in policy development. That might sound obvious in theory, but in practice, it may not be a straightforward process. If you are working on a policy that involves Constitutional rights, I recommend you seek advice from relevant authorities, like departments of justice or attorneys-general.

Amendments to the Constitution

The Constitution can only be amended by referendum through a majority vote of the Australian people. Since 1901, only eight out of the 44 referenda taken to the Australian people to change the Australian Constitution were supported.*

Takeaways

- The Australian Constitution is the (British Parliament's) founding document for Australia.
- The Constitution is the rules and rights book for Australia's authorising environment and its citizens.
- The Constitution establishes a hierarchy of governments with the Australian Government in the top seat, noting however that it can't jeopardise the states' independence. The territories however are not immune to their independence being jeopardised.
- There are three bodies with confirmed powers in each jurisdiction:
  - Parliaments have legislative power.
  - Executive governments have administrative powers.
  - Judiciaries have judicial power.
- The Constitution is underpinned by six principles — democracy, rule of law, separation of powers, federalism, nationhood and rights.

*Referenda are held only in relation to changes to the Australian Constitution. A plebiscite, yet again a different type of vote, is a vote of the Australian people on an issue of national significance but one that does not affect the Constitution. Australia has had four national plebiscites. Two were held during WWI to support conscription, neither of which was successful. 'Advance Australia Fair' won the day in the 1977 plebiscite for the choice of Australia's national song. The latest and successful plebiscite was in 2017 supporting legalising same-sex marriage.

Action steps

- Take time to become familiar with the complex document that is the Constitution.
- Actively look for examples in your work and in the media of the separation of powers.
- Whether you are preparing drafting instructions for legislation or developing policy, consider the interplay between your jurisdiction and that of the Commonwealth. And for those of you in the Commonwealth, consider this in light of the other Australian jurisdictions.
- When reviewing any policy, test it against the Constitution's six principles. Raise any doubts or concerns with your supervisor.

Chapter 5

The Westminster system — a glossary

In chapter 4, we had a good look at the British Parliament's founding document for Australia — the Australian Constitution. The Constitution describes how Australia is to be governed. Chapter 5 illustrates how the Constitutional model of governance is organised in the Westminster system, with its cornerstone of structure and order. Without the Westminster system, I could speculate that the Constitution might just be a document gathering dust on an archive shelf, or perhaps, even more speculation, it might be on display in a museum outside of the British Empire.

The Westminster system is the British system of parliamentary government by which the Commonwealth, including the nine governments in Australia (the total of the state, territory and federal governments), is governed. The Westminster system can appear unnecessarily complicated and archaic, and as such, chapter 5 strips the system back to its bones with a governance glossary I wish I had handy at the beginning of my policy career.

The Westminster system structure

The key components of the Westminster system are:

- A governor-general — or, in the case of the Northern Territory (NT), an administrator — who represents, in their jurisdiction, the unelected constitutional monarch (Australia's

Governor-General is also the constitutional monarch's representative in the ACT)

- A parliament which is both a physical place (that is, the nine parliament buildings in Australia) and the collective noun for parliamentarians — all elected members of a jurisdiction — who work to make and change their relevant jurisdiction's legislation, represent their constituents and keep check on what the government of the day is doing

- An executive government — more commonly known as the government or the government of the day — formed by the political party (or a coalition, an alliance of political parties forming government) that has the majority support following an election

- A first minister (for each government) who is elected as the leader by their political party. In the ACT, the Assembly is responsible for electing their first minister.

- The first minister of the Australian Government is the prime minister. For the states, the first minister is the premier; and the territories have chief ministers.

- Each government's first minister chooses their ministry from their party's or coalition parties' elected members. This means that not all elected members of the majority vote will automatically become ministers.

- Each minister is designated one or more portfolios of responsibility, for example disability services, police fire and emergency management, and innovation, science and the digital economy.

- The first minister and their ministers form a cabinet which is accountable to parliament. Each cabinet in Australia considers and determines matters such as government policy, national issues and legislation — keep in mind that only a parliament has the conferred power to legislate. It's interesting to note that the Australian Constitution does not refer to cabinets and that cabinets themselves have no legal power.

- A judiciary that is independent from both the elected parliament and the executive government. In Australia, the judiciary is made up of the High Court of Australia and other federal courts, for example, the Family Court of Australia. Each state and territory also has a judiciary. The states and territories have a supreme court and other state and territory courts, such as the Country Court of Victoria and the Magistrates Court of Tasmania.

- A public service comprising departments (sometimes referred to as agencies) that deliver services to the public (parks, emergency services and consumer affairs, to name a few) and drive the government of the day's policy objectives. Under the *Public Service Act 1999* (Cth), a key value of the Australian Public Service is that it "is apolitical and provides the Government with advice that is frank, honest, timely and based on the best available evidence".[1] This value is reflected across all state and territory public services.

Action steps

I only have one action for you: bookmark this chapter so you can easily find it when you are not sure who or what or how everything comes together in the Westminster system. After a while, you won't need to refer to it anymore. However, keep the bookmark in place so that you can easily share it with someone else who has been bamboozled by the Westminster system. I don't know about you, but I hear Westminster, and all I see are royal weddings…

Chapter 6

The machinery of government

You are part of a system called the machinery of government (commonly known as the MoG). Each MoG is shaped and structured by the Australian Constitution and the Westminster system that we considered in chapters 4 and 5 (remember, there are nine governments in Australia, which means there are nine MoGs). The MoG is how a government and its public service are structured and interconnected. It includes smaller-scale systems and processes such as governance as well as the allocation of functions and responsibilities between ministers and 'their' departments.

Changes to a MoG typically follow a general election, though a MoG change can also occur during a term of government. You are part of your government's MoG, and as you continue in your public service career, you will experience the highs and lows of many a MoG. If you don't work in a public service, your organisation and your sector will also feel the effects of MoG changes. Even a supposed innocuous change to a department name and structure can flip your world on its head. Staff, whole teams and service delivery can be moved to different departments, reduced or even discontinued as a result of MoG changes.

Before we focus on how general elections trigger a MoG change, we'll first consider other triggers — leadership spills, cabinet reshuffles, special cabinets, ministerial changes and the sacking of a prime minister.

The system

There has been a flurry of leadership spills in Australia in recent years that, by default, force a leadership resignation. When there is a leadership spill of a government's first minister, you can bet your socks there will be significant MoG changes. Not only will there be a new lineup of ministers (those who supported the new leader likely to be in favour, and those who supported the 'spilt' leader definitely out of favour), but also ministerial portfolios — for example, fisheries and veterans affairs — can change, be introduced, absorbed or, by the stroke of a pen, cease to exist.

Following a leadership change, it is also possible that there will be a complete shake-up of a public service, including a 'spill and fill' — when public servant positions are declared vacant, and new positions are created and advertised. So whether a public servant has been in their job for a long time or had just started, if they want to be considered for one of the new positions, they will need to apply.

A minister stepping down, being asked to step down, deciding to leave their party though remain in parliament, or having no choice but to step down immediately can also trigger a MoG change. If the minister who stepped down remains in parliament, the first minister will choose their replacement from existing elected members. If however a minister resigns — for example, in the case of stepping away from politics to give the next generation an opportunity to step up — or a minister is sacked, a bi-election will be held to fill the vacant seat in parliament (unless a minister's resignation comes into effect at the time of the next scheduled election).

Special cabinets can also impact a MoG. Australia has had two special cabinets. The first was formed in 1939 when former Prime Minister Robert Menzies created the War Cabinet, handpicking five senior ministers from his cabinet to join him. It became the key decision-making body in Australia throughout World War II. The War Cabinet was disbanded in 1945 with the return to peace.[1]

The second special cabinet, still in place today, is the National Cabinet that was established by the Council of Australian Governments "to coordinate and deliver a consistent national response to the Covid-19 pandemic".[2] The broader remit of National Cabinet reflects its ongoing relevance as a "genuine partnership between the Commonwealth and States and Territories on issues of national significance".[3] National Cabinet's decisions impact all governments' public services as the latter is responsible for coordinating and preparing a National Cabinet and implementing the decisions. You could well have an opportunity to be part of this — exciting!

However, the most infamous MoG change in Australia's political history was triggered by the sacking of former Prime Minister Whitlam. In a move that shook the nation to its core, then Governor-General Kerr dismissed Whitlam on 11 November 1975 and appointed Liberal leader Malcolm Fraser as the caretaker Prime Minister. In your action steps for this chapter, I have included a great book recommendation so you can learn about the Whitlam dismissal and the shockwaves that still reverberate today. But for now, let's shift our focus to MoG changes triggered by an election, namely:

- proroguing a parliament
- initiating caretaker mode
- choosing a cabinet
- the Administrative Arrangements Order
- changing public service structures, functions and responsibilities.

General elections and MoG changes

General elections, with mandatory voting in Australia's democracy, occur frequently at the federal, state, territory and local government levels. Australian Government elections are held every three years, and state, territory and local government elections are held every four years.* There are also by-elections, elections when a seat (or seats) becomes vacant in any government.

Before an election triggers a MoG change, a parliament needs to be prorogued — a catchy word that will get you a 14-point Scrabble© score — and thus the tides of change commence.

Choosing the next election date and proroguing a parliament

As the term of a government comes to an end within its prescribed time (see callout box), the first minister advises the relevant governor-general or administrator of their chosen election date. The governor-general or administrator usually dissolves the parliament by announcing a prorogation of parliament.**

When a parliament is prorogued, the next election is triggered. While ministers continue in office, parliamentary business (considering new laws for example) is ceased, and the caretaker conventions come into play. The announcement of an election in relation to a MoG is like the 'on your marks, get set' command without the starting gun being fired. The MoG starting gun will only be fired once the new or re-elected government is sworn in, rolls up its sleeves and gets stuck into governing.

*Interestingly, in England, the birthplace of the Westminster system, voting is not mandatory.

**Governors-general and administrators do have the reserve power to refuse a request to call an election, though it is rarely used. In 1909, Governor-General William Humble Ward did refuse a request to call an election when he commissioned Alfred Deakin as Prime Minister and asked him to form a coalition government after the government of the day lost the support of the majority of the House of Representatives.[4]

Caretaker conventions

Caretaker is the period between the prorogation of a parliament and the swearing-in of a new or re-elected government. While a parliament is dissolved, government business continues, and government maintains the administration of ordinary matters to ensure the relevant jurisdiction continues to run. Doctors and nurses keep caring, teachers keep teaching, health inspectors keep closing dodgy restaurants and the tax office keeps collecting taxes.

*There is one notable exception: National Cabinet continues to meet through state and territory caretaker periods, and may meet if the Australian Government is in caretaker and in accordance with caretaker conventions. [5]

However, during caretaker, a government is unable to implement major policy initiatives. That means it cannot announce the building of a new light rail for example, make appointments of significance (such as a new Australian ambassador), or enter into major contracts or undertakings (for example, a security agreement with Pacific Island leaders) unless it has the express support of the opposition government to do so.*

Why does this matter? First, the parliament has been prorogued. Second, the caretaker period recognises the potential for a change of government to occur following an election and the importance of not binding or limiting an incoming government to something it may not have agreed to. It's also useful to note that caretaker periods in Australia are a question of weeks, not months — whoever is elected to a parliament and to a government will quickly hit the start button on all government and parliamentary business.

What do public servants do during caretaker?

Public services, apolitical by nature, continue throughout a caretaker period to ensure their resources are not used in a manner that would advantage a political party or advance an issue (refer to the Westminster system, chapter 5). Public servants are issued caretaker conventions at the beginning of a caretaker period and are regularly reminded throughout that they are not to be involved or perceived to be involved in any election or political activities. Make sure you read the caretaker conventions cover to cover when they hit your desk or inbox. If you are unclear about anything, make sure you ask someone (who knows what they are talking about) to get the facts.

Like a parliament, a public service continues business as usual and attends to the administration of ordinary matters. Furthermore, and in accordance with caretaker requirements for parliaments, public servants cannot start to develop or prepare for new policy or legislation, commence contract or partnership negotiations, or actively engage with other state, territory or international governments or dignitaries. It is also common for communication with a department's minister's office to be limited to the most senior public servants.

While an election in one jurisdiction doesn't impose caretaker conventions on any other jurisdiction, it will slow government business between jurisdictions. For example, a jurisdiction 'in caretaker' is unable to represent their government's position and/or decision (because the government is in caretaker) at cross-jurisdictional meetings or during bi-partisan policy development unless it is agreed to by the opposition or National Cabinet has been called.

At first glance, caretaker might appear to be a significant decrease of workload. It isn't! There is much to prepare during caretaker additional to regular service delivery and paying government bills. A key focus for every department is the preparation of incoming briefs.* (*What's an incoming brief?!* I hear you cry.)

*Incoming briefs are but one type of brief public servants are required to prepare. Each government/ public service will have its own briefing nomenclature, however, there are briefs for hot issues.

Incoming briefs provide incoming ministers — some of whom may be returning ministers, others brand new ministers — with critical information to assist them with their duties. Keep in mind, large departments may have more than one minister. Incoming briefs 'introduce' each department to their minister(s) through strategic overviews, for example, advice about the relevant department's responsibilities, issues, opportunities, projects, policies, cross-government committees, initiatives and resources (staff, budgets, infrastructure). Incoming briefs will also detail legislative and regulatory requirements, including specific duties that can only be executed by the relevant minister and the relevant department or statutory authority.

(if you haven't guessed it, this is akin to a rollercoaster coming off its tracks), legislative assembly, cabinet, estimates, hearings, inquiries, royal commissions, cross-ministerial portfolio considerations, budget considerations — this list is long, very long...

Departments don't wait for the outcome of an election to prepare incoming briefs. Goodness, the incoming government wants to start business on day one and would not want to pop a 'closed until further notice' sign on the door while waiting on the lay of the land. Departments prepare two separate packs of incoming briefs — commonly, one in a blue book, the other in a red book that are ready to hit the desks of the incoming government on their first day of office.

(A quick style comment: I have intentionally not used uppercase in my list above as I am not referring to a specific cabinet or budget. Make sure you check your style guide so that you are applying the right style. It's extraordinary what turmoil an unnecessary or missing capital, or the incorrect use of a semicolon, can create!)

The blue book is for a new or re-elected liberal or coalition government, the red book for a new or re-elected labor government — both recognise the relevant party's policy agenda and election commitments. Regardless of which party or coalition that wins the election, it doesn't get a copy of the other party's or coalition's book. Each book also highlights important decisions that need to be made quickly because they have been on the backburner during caretaker. Another fun fact for you: the Australian Constitution does not recognise election commitments. The Australian Constitution only recognises decisions and commitments made by elected officials. Makes sense.

Incoming government

A new or re-elected government can also be referred to as the incoming government. It marks the line in the sand between the previous government and the shift to a government coming in (or returning) to power. The MoG changes' starting gun has been fired.

Choosing a cabinet

With each incoming government, there will be a new cabinet. Even for a returning government, it is not unusual to see changes in a cabinet's line-up. Prior to swearing in, the first minister will determine who will have a ministerial portfolio(s) and which of those ministers will be at 'their' cabinet table. In the Australian Government, the virtue of being chosen as a minister does not automatically mean a seat at the cabinet table. There is not a set size for a cabinet, and cabinets will differ from government to government and jurisdiction to jurisdiction.

Cabinets across parliaments in Australia serve as the administrative mechanism for the decision-making process of each executive government. Two interesting facts: first, Australian constitutions (the Australian Constitution as well as state and territory constitutions) do not explicitly provide for a cabinet, nor are cabinets recognised in any law.[6] Second, while cabinets are not recognised by law, cabinet confidentially is, and cabinet documents are expressly exempt under freedom of information laws. Generally, cabinet documents are protected for 10–30 years at which point they are released publicly. (It would be interesting for you to check the cabinet document protection period for your jurisdiction.) Cabinet documents are considered the property of the government of the day. An unauthorised or premature disclosure of a cabinet's documents, discussions and/or decisions is deemed to undermine the collective responsibility and authority of a cabinet.

If you are a public servant, make sure you read your government's cabinet handbook so that you understand the very strict cabinet processes and procedures that must be followed to the letter.

While cabinet can feel like a hundred miles away from your job, you will undoubtedly be involved in drafting documents for cabinet consideration, and you will certainly be impacted by cabinet decisions. (While you are looking for your government's cabinet handbook, also ask your supervisor/manager/team leader if you can do a MoG course — most worthwhile.)

Administrative Arrangements Order (AAO)

Each government has an AAO. Simply, an AAO is the government of the day's list of who is responsible for what. AAOs are adjusted to reflect an incoming government and kept updated during a term of a government to capture any ministerial, departmental and/or legislative changes. Always make sure you are referring to the most recent AAO version. AAOs are publicly available documents I find extremely useful. I encourage you to look up your AAO and keep abreast of all changes made to them.

Each AAO includes:

- the dated order made by the relevant governor-general or administrator
- the name of each department and the matters they deal with aligned to their minister(s)
- the legislation each department administers
- independent statutory authorities and their relevant legislation and regulation.

Some jurisdictions' AAOs will also include the title of the corresponding minister in relation to the above list. For those that don't, you can find ministerial responsibility listed on the relevant parliament's website. Each parliament website lists parliamentary members including those with a ministry and their corresponding portfolio responsibilities.

Changing public service departments' structures, functions and responsibilities

The consequences of MoG changes to public service are often disruptive, lengthy, costly and risky. In balance, however, MoG changes can be exciting, marking opportunities for needed evolution. MoG changes hold the promise of new beginnings, a turn of the tide, a long-awaited turning of the page. Time will tell if the promise blossoms into reality.

Though MoG changes are usually disruptive by nature, they are most disruptive post an election, even when what you have been hoping for has come to fruition. An incoming government is keen to wipe most if not all traces of the previous government (this can also occur when it's the same political party returning to power) and reposition a public service to meet the new policy priorities and agenda.

New departments can be established, and existing departments can be merged or even abolished. Positions, from the most senior public servants to those of junior staff, can be impacted. It's possible some may lose their jobs, some may be transferred to another team, and some may find themselves in a different role or department.

MoG changes can take months, if not years, to be fully realised.[7, 8] Redundancies, payouts, renaming, rebranding and physical relocation of departments often attract disapproval not only from an opposition government but also from both within and outside a public service.

At times, it can feel like MoG changes overshadow core public service business.

While MoG changes can happen in different ways, they are inevitable and very much part of being a public servant. My advice to you — just get on with it.

If you and your team have been working on a policy that gets shelved during a MoG change, that doesn't mean it is lost forever. Policies are a bit like the fashion trend carousel — they will ultimately come back, just like bell-bottomed jeans (who would have thought?). You also won't lose what you have learnt and developed. Your policy professional experience will always be in your policy kitbag, waiting for you to call upon it.

That said, you might also find your team's policy is suddenly in the spotlight. With that comes a new flurry of energy, direction, focus and (potentially) change. That is exciting stuff for us policy peeps, so enjoy it, ride that wave.

Whatever happens during a MoG change, the sooner you can settle into your new reality, the better. Let's face it, we can't change a MoG change, but we can always work towards developing *bloody good* policy.

Takeaways

- MoG changes can happen for a raft of reasons, and more often than not, a public service will experience changes as well.
- When an election has been called and the relevant governor-general or administrator has prorogued the parliament, the caretaker conventions come into play.

- Caretaker conventions impact what public servants can and cannot do.
- During caretaker, you will likely prepare incoming briefs — sharpen your pencils. And keep your pencils sharpened for all the other briefs you will write.
- The AAO is a great resource to identify ministers, departments and agencies' responsibilities including the legislation they administer.

Action steps

- Seek approval to do a MoG course — such a worthwhile investment!
- Make sure you are thoroughly versed in your jurisdiction's caretaker conventions.
- Bookmark your jurisdiction's AAO and always check that you have the most recent version, as an AAO can change during the term of a government.
- Be prepared for and adjust as quickly as you can to MoG changes. There's no disputing they can be hard, extraordinarily so, though we can't influence the changes. That said, they can be exactly what we were hoping for — which can be an adjustment too!
- Book club suggestion — Emeritus Professor and political commentator Jenny Hocking's two-volume biography on Gough Whitlam is a sensational read.
- If you're not up for a big read, settle down in front of the telly and watch the documentary about Jenny Hocking's commitment to uncover the truth behind the Whitlam sacking, *The Search For The Palace Letters*. It merits a chilled glass of something and perhaps some nibbles.

Chapter 7

The relationship between policy, legislation and regulation

Policy, legislation and regulation are closely aligned, and yet they have distinct differences. Their similarity lies in their shared purpose — to drive expected or desired behaviours to achieve specific goals. Their difference lies in their interdependence — how they can depend on each other, for different reasons. Another key difference is that legislation and regulation shape behaviours through rules and obligations that are administered and regulated by specific bodies, and for which there are consequences for non-compliance. Policies can also include rules to shape behaviours — for example, operational policy — however, policies don't always have rules.

Policy, legislation and regulation interdependence

For legislation and regulation to exist, they need a public policy first. I remember the day this was explained to me by a former NT Parliamentary Counsel. I couldn't believe my ears. At the time, I was trying to handball some work her way, which she most graciously declined because, as she put it, I needed to sort the policy first! *What?!* True story — the policy purpose, scope and parameters must be sorted for the drafters to do their bit — draft legislation and regulation for parliament consideration (remember, only parliaments have the power to make and change laws).

What an epiphany. So many things fell into place — and they all made policy even more exciting than what I thought it was. Remember our definitions of policy and legislation? Policy and legislation are peas in a pod — and for a fleeting moment, policy is the alpha pea. Clearly, legislation hops into the alpha seat once it has been passed by a parliament. However, legislation and regulation can't exist without policy. I love this.

How public policy, legislation and regulation influence each other — or not

As you know, public policy is generated by governments. Nevertheless, public policy is often born in the community (or, for the more sceptical of us, on the back of envelopes in shady bars) and shaped by our social contexts and fabrics. Policies for same-sex marriage, providing improved access to buildings for people with reduced mobility or a disability, food labelling and climate change were responses to an evolving society and were not initiated by those in government.

Public policy informs and positions the drafting, amending or rescinding of legislation and regulation by articulating their purpose, scope and parameters. All the examples in the above paragraph informed legislative change. In turn, legislation and regulation require policies to bring them into everyday considerations and activities, inside and outside governments and public services.

Let's take a closer look at an example regarding food safety to get a feel for the interplay between public policy, legislation and regulation.

Food safety legislation, regulation and policy

Let's have a look at how operational policy is required to ensure compliance with legislation and regulation. We'll look at the *Food*

Act 2003 (NSW) (the Act) and Food Regulation 2015 (NSW) (the regulations) as our examples.

This Act "regulates the handling of food for sale and the sale of food to provide for the application of the Australia New Zealand Food Standards Code in New South Wales".[1] The regulations ensure that in NSW, all food sold is safe and suitable for human consumption and meets all the Food Standard Code requirements.

Now think about a corner shop near you that sells fresh food, dried and tinned food, handy last-minute picnic things and alcohol. Let's say it also has a lovely deli section with salads, fancy pies and delicious, sweet delights.

To be able to open, stock and operate the corner store, the owner must comply fully with the Act and regulations including undergoing Food Safety Supervisor training. And let's face it, there are many more legislative and regulatory requirements for the shop — waste disposal, restricted trading days and signage display, to name a few.

For the corner shop's Food Safety Supervisor to ensure the shop's staff clearly understand what they must and must not do, the shop would have its own operational policies to guide staff. The operational policies would be the staff's go-to reference as to how to do their job — instead of having to wade through pages of legislation and regulation, which can be difficult to grasp without ample time and more than likely a legal interpreter on hand. Fortunately, the Australian Institute of Food Safety provides access to a range of guides, posters, templates, fact sheets and videos to support the shop owner and their staff.

It's not just organisations or small businesses that have operational policies to guide staff adherence to legislation and regulation. Government departments will also have similar operational policies to ensure their application of legislation and regulation, for example, the *Fair Work Act 2009* (Cth) that applies to all organisations and businesses and their jurisdictions' employment and management legislation, and financial management acts.* However, as you'll read about in a moment, policy can be developed without requiring legislation or regulation.

*No matter where we live in Australia, both Commonwealth and our jurisdiction's legislation will be in force, and all policies must be lawful — no Get Out Of Gaol Free card® for this.

When public policies and policies are not directly linked to legislation and regulation

While government departments are in the business of public policy, they also have many policies that are not a consequence of legislation and regulation.

Tourism is an important and valuable sector in Australia's economy, and every jurisdiction wants their share (if not the biggest share) of the tourism pie. It's not a legislative requirement to market Australia's many tourism destinations, though there is a lot of tourism public policy (and public funding) focussed on doing just that.**

**'Where the bloody hell are you?' was a campaign to drive Tourism Australia's policy goals to increase visitor numbers from Japan, Germany and the United Kingdom. Unfortunately, it didn't achieve its targets, with reports identifying visitor numbers had dropped from each of the target countries.

On the flip side, there is a stack (clearly not the legal term) of legislation and regulation with which the tourism industry, including tourism departments, must comply about how they market Australia's tourist destinations among many other things.

There are also public health promotions and initiatives that the public is not legally obliged to follow. We are often reminded, be that through direct correspondence, advertising campaigns or advice from health professionals, about the importance of making healthier choices. We are encouraged to have regular health checks, get cancer screening, stop smoking and lead a healthy and active life fuelled by a balanced diet and a good night's sleep. The driver here for governments is not to penalise citizens who do not follow public health advice — rather, the driver is the value (including the financial value) of preventing disease and promoting health versus the increasing costs of illness and disease not to mention the financial and social burden.

As members of the public, we are not obligated to access or use the outputs of all public policies. We aren't required to have a breast screen or to holiday in Australia, nor are we required to send our kids to a public school or ignore the iced coffee with whipped cream and chocolate sprinkles at the hospital's cafeteria (though the temptation is strong) and grab some water instead. These are examples of policies that are not directly linked to legislation and therefore do not have legal or regulatory consequences for non-adherence.

Let's briefly go back to the owner of your corner store. They too may have policies that aren't linked to legislation and regulation. For instance, they may have a policy to support one of the local sports teams by providing fresh fruit at all their local matches. They may also have a policy to support local producers by promoting and stocking their products. Neither of these policies are driven by legislation and regulation, rather, they are driven by the store owner's fabulous community spirit.

Legislation without regulations

A brief note here about legislation not always requiring regulations. Regulations aren't always required for legislation, for example, legislation across Australia regarding the age of majority does not have specific regulations. However, some of us may be required to prove our age for entry into a club or bar (I remember those days — both needing to prove I was old enough for entry and actually going out to clubs and bars!), as are licensed premises required to seek proof from us.

Takeaways

- Policies, legislation and regulation are closely knitted together and often rely on one another to exist.
  - Legislation requires a public policy to shape its purpose, parameters and focus.
  - Laws often, though not always, need regulations and a regulator to ensure compliance.
  - Laws bring into play the very public policies that shaped them.
- A public policy that has shaped legislation is put into action when the legislation is passed. It starts and ends with policy — the circle of life!
- Not all public policy is directly linked to legislation and regulation, though all policies must be lawful.
- Different types of policy (most notably operational policies) help organisations, businesses and government departments apply legislation and regulation.

Action steps

- Have a look at the Australian Government's Office of Parliamentary Counsel that provides a fabulous resource to learn more about the drafting of legislation.[2]
- Start to make simple maps identifying the relationships

between and across the policies you are working on with legislation and regulation.

- Identify from whom you can get advice to understand how legislation and regulation need to be considered to ensure your policy work is in accordance with the relevant legislative and regulatory framework.

Part 3:

How to be a *bloody good* policy officer

It's about human being, not human doing.
Ben Crowe 2023 (The Imperfects)

In Part 3, I want to share with you what I learnt from observing and working with some amazing people. My focus here is not how to **do** *bloody good* policy work (though they definitely taught me that too — and we'll cover this in Part 4), but rather how they taught me the essence of how to **be** a *bloody good* policy officer.

Working in policy is like riding a rollercoaster. To this day, I experience each policy as a wrestle with gravity that leaves me disoriented, dishevelled, discombobulated — and wanting more. Sometimes we're riding the rollercoaster highs and lows with allies, at other times with foe. Regardless of with whom we are working or the resources we can access, we must remain committed to developing a policy that takes people (or people and things) from where they are now to where an organisation or a government wants them to be.

Policy development is dynamic. It constantly responds to and influences its environment. It's full of change, conflicting opinions, leadership shakeups and shifting priorities. Policy development can be hard and incredibly confronting, though rewarding, work. Hence, policy is not for everyone.

It's *who you are* that's the point of difference between a *bloody good* policy officer and those for whom policy is just a job. It's how we navigate policy by the three sources of wisdom — our heads, hearts and guts — that makes the distinction.

Bloody good policy officers understand policy through their senses. They see, hear and empathise with the people who will be impacted by a policy and how those people experience the world around them. *Bloody good* policy officers hear what people are saying and can read between the lines, too. They celebrate joys and breakthroughs. They care if people are suffering, are constrained, considered as different, are ignored, persecuted. They recognise that competing, even conflicting, laws and policies are often the sources of wicked policy problems — not the people who will be impacted by a policy.

So, what's the profile of a bad policy officer? The people who tend to flounder or even fail in policy are those who are template pushers and fillers, plodding through processes until knock-off time. Or they are the controllers: those who mask their own fear or lack of policy knowledge by blocking the wisdom and guidance of experts and those with lived experience, stubbornly ignoring the opportunities and possibilities they offer. Or they just don't care about what they are doing. Please don't work in policy if it's only a paycheque to you. Please don't work in policy if you are not driven by the wellbeing of others. The people and things for whom policy is developed deserve much more than that.

Fortunately, over my career I've learnt from many incredibly effective policy officers and leaders from both government circles and other sectors. I will introduce you to 10 of these wonderful people in chapter 8.

In chapter 9, we are going to do some bellybutton gazing. When we work in policy, it's important to know what drives us and what shapes, if not clouds, our judgement. It's equally important to recognise those parts of policy we are comfortable to work in, the parts that challenge us, and the parts that stretch us way out of our comfort zone.

In chapter 10, we'll turn our attention to the constantly changing dynamic that is the realm of policy. We'll consider how we must quickly recognise and adapt to changes in our social fabric, and how those changes may impact and influence our policy work. I think it's time for another cuppa, and why not try some different biccies?

Chapter 8

Bloody good **policy officer cameos**

In this chapter, I share with you 10 cameos of some of the people who inspired me and helped me work out how to become a *bloody good* policy officer. They are not fearless; they are courageous. They don't seek the spotlight; they shine the light where it is needed. They don't need to be right; they fight for the rights of those who are or will be impacted by policy. They don't want to have the last word; they champion the voices of others. They bring policy to life; they make change possible through the informed advice they provide decision makers. They rejoice when the 'right' policy works; they don't give up when it doesn't.

Their stories below are snapshots of *who they are* as opposed to how skilled they were at a certain task, such as policy writing. You can always learn new skills, and rest assured, you will learn many while working in policy. However, skills alone won't make you a *bloody good* policy officer. It is who you are, as well as who and what you care about, that will. It's about being in policy to make a difference for those who seek your help to drive change.

Let me introduce you to some wonderful people.

Nell

Nell introduced me to the power of three things —

- genuine stakeholder engagement
- flat and factual advice (aka frank and fearless, and truth to power — see chapter 10)
- competently navigating the unpredictable relationships between a government and its public service.

Nell taught me that humanity should be at the heart of every policy. She taught me that policy impacts people's lives — and not always for the better. Nell taught me the importance of taking the time to be with people, to learn about and from them, and to listen to their stories about how policies touched their lives, their families, neighbourhoods and communities. Nell taught me that for policy to be effective and drive the desired change, we must always engage with those people who are and will be affected by what we do.

Nell doesn't distort information to suit a political or personal narrative. She doesn't imply, ignore or try to fill in gaps from what she has learnt. Nell understands the long-term value of providing flat and factual policy advice — in the best interest of the public, not tailored to suit a particular narrative, and that doesn't risk diluting if not distorting the value of a policy.

I began to understand the fraught (and at times fickle) relationship between a government and its public service when I worked with Nell. Nell helped me to understand and navigate political drivers, incentives and even interference in policy work. Nell's practical and pragmatic advice helped me to identify when I could influence political and public service tensions (relevant to the work I was doing) and those that I couldn't. In fact, she provided me a manual of how to navigate the complexity of government and public service relationships. Her manual's key message through all of this is "flat and factual, frank and fearless, truth to power" — every single day.

Eve

The most important thing I learnt from Eve is that no matter how scary giving flat and factual advice can be, there is no excuse to shy away from it. Eve lives and breathes integrity, and she weaves it through everything she does. This takes courage, as it can lead to consequences you might find surprising (unless you've been around the block a few times and have seen this play out). Not everyone is open to flat and factual guidance. What they don't understand is that Eve is a problem solver, not a blocker.

Eve's motivation is to provide evidence-informed advice to inform decision making. She understands risk and risk appetite. She is cautious when required and advises confidently when different approaches or possibilities are doable. She is not a 'whatever goes' person — she checks, thoroughly. She won't let a lackadaisical approach to process and procedure stuff up policy.

Eve doesn't shy away from asking questions, especially the uncomfortable ones. She asks questions to create a pause for others to reflect, to consider, to double check, to do the right thing. And she'll call it if the right thing is not being done — even if it means risking her own career. She has a sixth sense of knowing when something is missing or not right or at complete odds with governance, policy or legislative frameworks. She is not officious. She is welcoming, caring, kind, considerate and ever so patient.

Eve's purpose is to protect the integrity of each and every policy. Everyone impacted by policy (let's face it — that's all of us) deserves an Eve looking out for them.

Evan

Evan was the first data expert to ask me about the stories behind, and generated by, policy. I love stories. However, I find the number gig overwhelming, and I'll often switch off when people dig into a number conversation. Evan made me realise that although we speak different languages, we share the same purpose.

Evan and I swap numbers and stories to build policy pictures. I started to experience policy in a completely different way. I felt like a kid playing an old-fashioned card swap game (minus the bubble gum and a picture of an American baseball player in the packet). We support our policy stories (qualitative data) with numbers (quantitative data) and vice versa. We call it when the numbers don't support our hypothesis; this paves the way for us to explore alternative pathways. We look for different indicators and explore proxy data, variables and time series.

I now have a vocabulary that expands my ability to communicate and engage with a much broader audience (i.e., stakeholders). My number abilities only go so far, but with Evan by my side (and all the other wonderful Evans I have been blessed to work with), so many more opportunities open up for me to identify policy solutions and possibilities. It also sets us up beautifully for review, monitoring and evaluation. That's policy magic right there.

Les

When I talk with Les (actually, it's better if I just sit back and listen), I'm taken on a journey that weaves its way through the past, what tomorrow could look like, and how today reflects both. I imagine Les' mind as a never-ending library wherein every shelf holds a new treasure trove of political, social and public history.

Les' understanding of the machinery of government, systems, processes, governance, policies and political dramas is second to none. His ability to share his knowledge is inspirational. He can quickly spot gaps of knowledge, understanding or appreciation of the order of events and then, through ongoing discussions, he generously fills those gaps without being condescending, overpowering or dismissive.

I always feel very smart after a conversation with Les — I'm literally glowing with my newfound knowledge and understanding. Les has taught me the importance of sharing information (he is the antithesis of hoarding knowledge as a power play), genuinely listening to learn, and the absolute necessity for us to value the wisdom of First Nations knowledge holders and to respect their knowing, being and doing.

Griff

Fact 1: Policy amounts to nothing if it can't be implemented.

Fact 2: We need to embed implementers (the people who will implement a policy, i.e., service delivery, program rollout) from the very beginning of every policy journey.

Fact 3: Implementers know so much stuff that we policy officers don't.

Fact 4: We know all the above facts, and yet we still struggle to get implementation right.

Enter Griff. Griff is one of those rare operators who has a deep knowledge, understanding and expertise of frontline service delivery, policy and strategic leadership. He has worked in urban, regional and remote settings, and across different sectors. He can talk the talk and walk the walk. He is the frontline champion. His favourite questions go something like this:

- How will this work on the ground?
- How do you know?
- Who did you talk to?
- Did everyone agree?
- Do they believe it can be done?
- How do they know?
- How will you know if it has been done?
- What's the backup plan if it doesn't work?
- Who is going to benefit from it?
- Who isn't?

Straightforward, no-nonsense questions. But my goodness, things can and do go pear-shaped if we don't take the time to ask them and actually do something with the responses.

I had the wind taken out of my sails the first time Griff hit me with his questions. I couldn't answer them, and I realised with shame (and that wasn't his intention) that I hadn't considered implementers, nor had I considered how we would know if a policy was working or not. Now I always ask myself, *What would Griff want to know?*

Alex

I first met Alex during a job interview. I was the chair; she was the interviewee. I was struck by three things — her experience, her ability to be present in the interview (she listened, considered, shared) and her gentle calmness. Much later, she would tell me she died a thousand deaths during that interview, convinced she had done it all wrong. To the contrary, Alex was exactly what we needed.

My team at the time was boisterous, to put it mildly. We were out to save the world, convinced we could slay all the baddies and crown humanity in all its glory. We were giddy with excitement and hopeful 'what ifs', and we were shouting it out to the world. Rookie mistake… and by then, I wasn't a rookie.

Alex sits back. She listens and then listens some more. She researches purposefully, synthesises and analyses data and prepares her advice before sharing it. When Alex speaks, we stop and listen.

Alex has the facts; she knows the strengths and weaknesses of our policies. She knows who needs what advice, and how we need to prepare policy advice so that it grabs our decision makers' and stakeholders' attention. She knows how to present information to decision makers and stakeholders in a format to support their deliberation and decision-making processes. Providing decision makers with the information they need as opposed to what they want is an important line in the sand we need to draw.

Alex is an influencer — a key part of *being* in policy. She taught me so much, starting with not needing to be the first person to talk in the room or to even talk at all. Powerful stuff.

Yash

There are many wonderful people who are the backbone of policy teams. They provide support, they make things happen, they help tidy up our messes (and no, I'm not referring to my desk), they always seem to be there ready to help. Yash is one of these people. Though the way Yash really helps us is through their storytelling.

Let me rewind. When Yash started with us, they were quiet. They observed the way we worked together, the way we supported each other. Little by little, their confidence grew in us, as did their confidence to be their true self with us. And then they started to share their stories.

Yash's stories are about their childhood — the excitement of going bush to pick rosellas (even more excited about eating the jam); their huge family full of kids, aunties and uncles, all characters with an abundance of love, laughter and extraordinary stories of survival; of Northern Australia during World War II, of the Stolen Generations, of so much more. Yash's stories lift our heads from our computer screens, remind our guts what our purpose is, and open our hearts to humanity. Yash makes policy real.

Helena

Helena works in the Aboriginal Community Controlled Sector. I can't imagine how many public servants Helena has seen come and go; my guesstimate is hundreds.

Helena is a highly respected expert in her sector. She has a clear understanding of which policies are effective, which aren't and where there are gaps, opportunities and waste. In short — she knows her stuff. I first met Helena at a time when there was significant Australian and Northern Territory government focus on and investment in her sector. Helena and her colleagues were invited to endless focus groups and meetings.

I had not long started in this particular job when I met Helena at what was just another government meeting to add to her tally. I thought I was well prepared for the meeting. The look on Helena's face as I introduced myself and stated the purpose of our meeting told me, very pointedly, that I wasn't. Helena and her colleagues had been at countless of these meetings, told the same stories, shared the same data, provided practical and pragmatic solutions; there was no need to start this all over again.

What I learnt quickly from Helena was that being prepared to engage with stakeholders isn't just about what I want to say and do. Being prepared involves doing our homework to understand the drivers, motivations and experiences of our stakeholders.

Helena made sure I didn't forget this critical step for every single meeting I go to. And I am forever grateful.

Bernie

Like Yash and Helena, Bernie makes policy real — kicked-in-the-guts real. Bernie lives and breathes the reality and consequences of policy — the good, the bad and the shockingly ugly. Bernie has worked in frontline service delivery for years, and no one knows it better than him.

Bernie is a gentle giant. His heart takes on all the hurt of those he professionally cares for. There doesn't seem to be a limit as to how much he can bear, for how long he can try to make every day that little bit better, how often he tries to shift heaven and earth to let rays of sunshine get through to those who need it most.

You don't get through a life of this type of professional commitment without bruises, scars and a broken heart. Every now and then, I catch glimpses of how much policy, and truly ghastly policy, costs Bernie. The tears of children bruise him, their broken bodies scar him. His heart shatters as he knows that too often there is only one direction these kids can take, forever damaged by heartless policies.

And yet, Bernie turns up every day, hopeful that the tide will finally turn and that people will see these kids for what they are — kids. They desperately need love, shelter, belonging, understanding, protection and hope. Every day, Bernie leaves disappointed. However, he is always there the next morning with a smile on his face, a skip in his step and his heart full of hope for the kids.

Bernie taught me to never give up. Keep going until you turn that tide for good. And if you can't, get out of the way so someone else can.

Thea

When we are a *bloody good* policy officer, we either find the *bloody good* policy teams — or they find us!

We all have stories about the leaders we utterly enjoyed working with, those who were so-so and those who don't deserve a mention. I've been very lucky to have worked for a handful of leaders who gave purpose, direction and meaning to our work. In wrapping up this chapter, I'd like to share with you what I learnt from one of my favourite leaders, Thea.

When I worked for Thea, I woke up every morning energised and excited to embrace the day. I knew I was going to be challenged and supported, stretched and protected, and I knew I was respected and appreciated.

Being part of Thea's team was my version of getting picked for the major league. She has a wonderful ability to bring together diverse people with different backgrounds and expertise united by a shared purpose and values. She brought in other experts and engaged with people with lived experience to fill the gaps of knowledge and understanding that we missed in our team. We learnt together and from each other, we challenged each other, we galvanised each other.

Thea created a safe environment where we could have robust debates, reflect, pause, start again, take a different pathway or stick to our course. She understood when we needed time out and insisted on it when we were too stubborn to let go. She jumped into the unknown with us or encouraged a solo leap of faith when she knew what we didn't — that we could do it. Thea celebrated and commiserated with us.

Thea was our leader, ally and champion. As our gifted leader, she shared with us a desire to be a better follower, and to achieve better outcomes for the people impacted by our policy work.

Every once in a while in the field, you'll recognise leaders like Thea, and if you're lucky, you'll get to work for them. Work hard to be a *bloody good* policy officer, and there's a good chance the *bloody good* leaders will find you first.

Takeaways

- Policy is so much more than a skill set — though you'll learn many (and transferable) skills in your policy roles.
- At its core, policy is about people; we need to care about how people will be impacted by the policies we are working on.
- We can learn a lot about how to be a *bloody good* policy officer from others, including people who aren't in policy.
- Sometimes we need to recognise that we have done all we can and that it's time to let someone else step in and take over the ropes.

Action steps

- Be honest with yourself about why you work in policy.
- Find your policy voice by listening to your head, heart and gut.
- Don't be afraid to challenge the status quo. It can be scary, but the consequences of staying silent are often much worse.
- Working in policy is a privilege — make it matter, make it count.

Chapter 9

Where did I come from?

Where did I come from?[1] is a book that became the talk of the town when I was entering that awkward period for everyone involved — puberty. It was touted as "help[ing] generations of parents talk honestly with their children about the intimate world of human sexuality. An age-appropriate voice respectful of young people's natural intelligence and light-heartedly illustrated throughout". My 11-year-old natural intelligence told me that all the adults had gone mad and that essential social barriers between old people (anyone not in a school uniform) and 'us' had been mortifyingly breached. As for the *light-hearted* illustrations — they blew my little mind. That said, hidden away from outrageously embarrassing conversations with our parents and guardians, my friends and I went back time and time again to that book and those that followed. Very insightful.

Why oh why am I talking to you about this book? Because the question in the title is relevant to *who we are* as policy officers. Park the puberty stuff for the moment. (Unless of course you have kids and need some back-up; then I'd recommend you grab the whole series. Saves time and angst for everyone.)

Back to the question and variations of it. *Where did I come from? What's happening to me now? What has happened to me? Why do I think and behave in certain ways in certain situations? Who am I?* (Also another title in the above series.) In this chapter I want you to do some navel gazing (no need to go any further). I want you to put your analytical skills to good work, and I want you to ask yourself questions. And then I want you to honestly answer those questions — some ought to be difficult, even uncomfortable, to answer.

The purpose of these questions is to recognise that who we are, where we came from, and how our personal and professional experiences have shaped us will influence consciously and subconsciously:

- how we engage with others
- how we listen
- what we choose to hear
- how we build projections of what we expect will happen
- what we actually want to happen and why
- how we build perceptions of others
- how we weigh our value against others'.

This chapter provides an example of how we can influence policy development, and then it focuses on biases and assumptions. This time, instead of putting actions at the end of the chapter, I have included them under each section. Please do yourself a favour: cultivate a greater awareness of who you are and how you consciously and subconsciously influence your policy development. We may mean well, but we can inadvertently have a negative influence. Let me give you an example.

When I was working in youth justice, we had the opportunity to craft — alongside a fabulous, diverse array of stakeholders — a new youth justice strategy. It was a time like no other I had experienced. It was a promise of change, of completely flipping the approach from penalising kids. We wanted kids to be actively supported so they could understand what had happened to them and how they had reacted to the very ordinary life-dish they had been served. We wanted to engage *their* heads, hearts and guts to find hope, to find a future, to find themselves. In my excitement, I consciously blocked out all the things and people that came my way with opposing views — including the authorising environment.

The consequence? The complete reverse of what the collective 'we' were committed to achieving. I was providing policy advice though I had curated it to dilute, deflect and distract attention from some community voices that our approach was the opposite of what was needed. It wasn't my job to dilute, deflect or distract.

My job was to provide flat and factual, frank and fearless advice (more about the four Fs in the next chapter) so the authorising environment could make an informed decision. Perhaps things would have been different if I hadn't been so doggedly determined. I will never know. Here's the career-defining lesson I learned: had I understood how my behaviours, reactions, responses and approaches would influence (positively and negatively) the authorising environment and therefore the policy, I would have been doing the work of a *bloody good* policy officer.*

One more thing before I set you on your journey of self-discovery. I want to share with you what the policy officer rollercoaster *feels* like. Prepare to be thrown into the tripes of the policy development definition from chapter 1. It's messy.

Policy development is innately human. It is deeply personal for everyone involved. We blatantly scrutinise people's lives. We stand in the shadows, observing, listening, analysing. We bring people together to gather as allies, sometimes as foe.

The contradiction that is policy development is a gut-wrenching pull and push between constraint and liberation, alignment and disruption. Policy development can put the brakes on, and it can re-inject enormous energy into life. It is joyous, heart-wrenching, soul-

*When you know that an authorising environment is making decisions likely to cause harm or are outside the law, including international obligations and human rights, you **must** speak out. It's your duty whether you are a policy officer or not. If you ever have to go down this path, document everything, and make sure you have all the support you need.

destroying. Some celebrate our work, some are left behind, others lose hope, others resigned to give us another go.

The policy development dogs of war rage at our heels and tear away old wounds, leaving us bleeding and exposed. The policy development gods remind us that to give is to take away. And yet… with every single policy, there is hope and opportunity.

Hope that we can tease the threads of society's fabric to create something better, careful to not heedlessly disrupt. We remove the thorns, re-stitch worn and broken threads. We unite the new with the old, re-weaving the fabric of society to create new relationships and shape new or different behaviours. And we must never forget that each thread is a person, a family, a community, messy human relationships, and also us. As we're in the thick of policy development, we need to understand who we are. Take the time to ponder this.

Over to you now. It's time to consider how your biases and assumptions can influence the policy developments you work on and then do the allocated task. Capture one bias and one assumption now. (I know you don't want to put *Rollercoaster* down, but you will come back to it!) Then, every time a policy hits your desk, I want you to do them again specifically in relation to 'that' policy. It's quite extraordinary what you will discover. Over time, you will build a deep understanding of who you are, and you will be able to recognise when you need to dial up or down your behaviours, reactions, attitudes. Why is this important? Because we do influence the policies we are working on, and therefore we influence those who matter most — the people directly impacted by the policies we are developing. Are you ready?

Biases

The Macquarie Dictionary defines bias as "a particular tendency or inclination, especially one which prevents unprejudiced consideration of a question" and to "influence, usually unfairly; prejudice, warp". The senses for bias provided in the Macquarie Thesaurus are telling — *discrimination, inclination, lopsidedness, prejudice (misestimation), tare, warp, manipulate*. That's quite a lot of disarming senses.

On many an occasion, a policy task has hit my desk to which my initial response was along the lines of *WTF*. I've also had many an occasion when my response was, *About time, this is just what we wanted*. What I came to realise, and what behavioural experts will no doubt explain, is that our instinctual reactions to things will influence how we approach them. And this is absolutely true for policy development. I have dug my heels in when I have disagreed with a decision maker's policy agenda. I have also moved heaven and earth to get a policy I supported over the line. What's the problem with this? Well, to be a *bloody good* policy officer, we need to treat every policy task with transparency, accountability and honesty.

The simplest way to start is just by writing down our biases.

Your task

Make a list of your biases, tuck it away somewhere, and reread it every now and then. Don't forget to repeat this exercise with every policy task you work on, and regularly check that your biases aren't impacting your work.

Task purpose

Your awareness of your biases will increase, and you will be better positioned to manage them so that, as a *bloody good* policy officer, you can continue to provide frank advice without fear or favour (aka truth to power).

I was in the full throes of a bias when I was writing *Rollercoaster* — it happened to coincide with the 2024 US presidential race. I was one of millions of people around the world who were watching the race closely. I outwardly expressed my bias by immediately dismissing anything one of the candidates said and by condemning all of their actions. As a distant observer of this political race, perhaps my biases weren't that problematic. For the sake of example, let's superimpose my bias onto a situation in which I am developing policy. My bias would significantly restrict, if not completely consume, my ability to:

- provide flat and factual advice
- constructively listen and fully understand policy positions and their drivers
- identify opportunities to inform policy development.

So you can see, my bias would wipe out any aspiration I had to be a *bloody good* policy officer.

By the very nature of their job, public servants work with politicians. There will be times when the politicians really get under our skin — and you know what else? We can get under theirs! Public servants must be able to manage their biases to do their job effectively and serve the public.

Assumptions

Back to the trusty Macquarie Dictionary (I love a good dictionary). An assumption is:

1. "the act of taking for granted or supposing
2. "something taken for granted; a supposition
3. "the act of taking to or upon oneself
4. "arrogance; presumption".

The Macquarie Thesaurus (thesauri are a blast too) throws in *credence, embarkation, insolence* (ouch) and *reasoning* into the mix.

Recognising our assumptions and writing them down, as we did with biases, is critical.

Many moons ago, I worked in a friend's pub. One of my work buddies, Winnie, was the dishwasher. Winnie was Chinese, had not been long in Australia and had very little English. We struck a friendship that was built on facial expressions, gestures and lots of laughter. Winnie was learning English, and over the time we worked together, her English went from strength to strength. On one of our breaks, she told me she was a civil engineer and had come to Australia to make a better life. She was hopeful her family would be able to follow. I just about fell off my chair — I had assumed that Winnie's life, skill set and aspirations were restricted to what I saw at the pub. How wrong I was.

Imagine if I were working on a policy and I made assumptions about the people who would be impacted, people I didn't know or knew little of. There is a whopper of a chance the policy wouldn't even get close to driving the change. There is an even greater chance the policy would be harmful.

A weird thing happens in our brain (we are wired to the negative for the pure purpose of survival — though I don't know how Winnie being a civil engineer could have endangered my survival) when assumptions morph into beliefs. Dangerous, dangerous territory. We need to check our assumptions regularly, and you can start now.

Your task

The next time you listen to, watch or read your favourite media source, pay attention to any story that grabs your attention and to which you have a reaction. Write down every assumption you have about the story. You will do the same with each of your policy tasks.

The next step is to research the media story/policy to check to see if there is any evidence behind your assumptions. Make a table to take note of the assumption, and then park it if there is no evidence to back it up. If, on the other hand, you find evidence to support the assumption (which by default is no longer an assumption), add the following to your table:

- Start to build your evidence base* by documenting it. There's nothing worse than trying to find a paper or interview transcript that you read once but forgot to write down who wrote it, the title etc.
- Capture other useful evidence that you come across in your research —including the evidence that deep down you wish wasn't there.

*An evidence base (this is different to *evidence-based*) is not one single research paper or one solitary discussion/interview. Make sure you have triangulated (multiple sources of evidence), quantitative (numeric) and qualitative (narrative) data. Now you are building an evidence base — a very important distinction from cherry-picking evidence.

Task purpose

You will gain clarity between assumption and evidence. You will start to build a regular behaviour or response — to check not only your own assumptions but to also research what other people share with you throughout a policy development. It's an essential habit, indeed skill, to master.

Takeaways

- It's impossible to remove our true selves from our work — we are who we are, and we will influence in some way the work we are involved with.
- Biases and assumptions can and do shape our worldviews and opinions, and they create obstacles that cloud our judgement and understanding.
- Noting the two above points, it's important to understand and recognise how we can influence, perhaps unconsciously, different situations because of who we are. This in turn can impact those who matter most — the people directly impacted by the policies we develop.
- If we actively check in with ourselves, and if we are conscious of where our biases and assumptions can creep in and how we can manage them, we have a much better chance of being a *bloody good* policy officer.

Action steps

- Keep checking in on your biases and assumptions.
- Find someone with whom you are comfortable sharing your assumptions and biases. You can help each other identify any telltale signs of letting a bias or assumption get in the way of

you being a *bloody good* policy officer. Just make sure you don't fall into the trap of group think – i.e., a shared bias doesn't make it factual!

- See if you can recognise biases and assumptions in others. Don't just call them out on it; think of constructive ways of helping them consider different realities and see the bigger picture. For instance, you could:
  - share data with them
  - recommend they listen to other people's stories
  - share how you identified your biases and assumptions, and how by recognising them, you ensure they don't affect your work.

Chapter 10

The policy phoropter

If you have had your eyes tested, then you would have been asked to look through a phoropter. A phoropter is an ophthalmic testing device that slides over your eyes and ears, just like reading glasses. Phoropters allow optometrists to spin through multiple lenses to find the right correction for you, if indeed you require glasses. If you're not sure what I'm referring to, look them up, they're very cool.

Chapter 10 is about the policy phoropter. The latter will shift your focus from assumptions and biases to seeing the world around you through seven critical policy lenses which are, in no particular order:

1. curiosity
2. empathy
3. humanity
4. flat and factual / frank and fearless / truth to power
5. rigour
6. practical and pragmatic
7. courage.

We won't always meet, see, know, talk to or hear from all the people who will be impacted by the policies we are working on. The impact of policies is experienced across the geographical, political, economic and social dimensions of a jurisdiction, including the whole country and even beyond. Sometimes, it can feel like we are light-years removed from the effects of a policy. At other times, our policy work will hit home, directly impacting us or someone close to us. The policy phoropter's seven lenses will make sure we don't lose or dilute our focus on what's important to every single policy — people.

The seven lenses are directly linked to our definition of policy — "a change that takes people (or people and things) from where they are now to where an organisation or a government wants them to be". Regardless of what sector you work in or what type of policy you are working on, every single policy will have people at its core. People:

- decide what the policy agenda is
- develop policy
- contribute to policy
- implement policy
- evaluate policy
- hate, love, don't care, sometimes don't know about the myriad of policies that impact them directly and indirectly throughout their entire lives — from inception to the grave.

You have nearly read *Rollercoaster* in its entirety. You have learnt much along the way, perhaps returning to different parts of *Rollercoaster* to read them again and consider them from a different perspective. You have played with the action steps. Maybe you've done all the suggestions in the action steps (in that case, give yourself a gold star!). Perhaps you're creating new behaviours, new habits. You're on the cusp of doing *bloody good* policy work. Chapter 10 is the last piece to click into place.

Let's kick off with curiosity, which is the lifeblood of a *bloody good* policy officer.

Lens I — curiosity

Curiosity is the fuel for everything we do. Humans hunger to learn more. We are driven to understand others. We search relentlessly (as much as time permits) to listen, read, question, explore, analyse and synthesise all the evidence we can gather. *Bloody good* policy officers are genuinely curious.

Our curiosity needs to be tempered by sensitivity, awareness and understanding. We must be careful not to assume people will want to share their stories, lived experience, or even their time with us. We must also be acutely aware of not harming people by seeking their engagement. By that I mean we must not trigger difficult and traumatic experiences. We must never assume that our curiosity will always be welcome, however, our curiosity must always be genuine. And our curiosity openly invites people to give us feedback about our work, the direction a policy is taking, what it's missing, what it needs.

How to be curious

Perhaps curiosity does not come naturally to you. Perhaps you are more of a behind-the-scenes operator, comfortable with desktop research to discover what you need to know. Or you might be comfortable and skilled at connecting with a diverse range of people. You may well be a natural at both! If you are reading this and thinking, *My goodness, none of this is ringing any bells*, I have two questions for you.

First, can you commit to cultivating your curiosity? If yes, great — start building. Second, do you really want to be in policy? If no, then good on you for recognising it, however, I strongly recommend you find a job that suits you better. Staying in policy would not be fair to you or the people who will be impacted by the policies you would have worked on.

If you're committed to policy and to being curious, let's keep going! Below are some simple ways to harness your curiosity.

- Identify how you prefer to gather information. Is it by actively participating in stakeholder engagement, or observing stakeholder engagement? Do you prefer secondary research such as desktop research and ploughing through databases of peer-reviewed academic papers, or do you prefer getting out in the field to conduct primary research? Is it a mix of all of these or something else?
- Share the above with your colleagues/supervisor to identify your strengths and areas for you to develop.
- Ask if you can shadow someone (this means observe them doing their work) fulfilling their curiosity bent in a different way to you. For example, if you prefer primary research in the field, ask someone how they approach desktop research for something they know nothing about. Take notes, and then sit down at the computer and open up a research database. How mind-blowing is it to have a wealth of information at the tips of your fingers?
- Roleplay being curious in different settings. You might like to imagine you are in a stakeholder session and you have prepared two questions to ask. Imagine yourself asking the questions, the stakeholders answering, and surprising yourself by asking follow-up questions.
- Do your homework before all stakeholder engagement. What can you find out about them? What are they are keen to see happen in policy? What are they are most fearful of? This is a powerful exercise.
- Drink a full cup of courage and give it a shot — you'll be surprised at just how hungry your inner curiosity is!

Lens 2 — empathy

Empathy is the appreciation for and understanding of someone else. Sometimes, empathy can come naturally — we 'get' someone or a group of people. At other times, we need to work at truly considering someone else, for example, your minister, an advocate lobbying against or for a policy, a citizen who is in desperate need of change, someone who lives in a completely different 'world' to you. Why is empathy important? Empathy is the antidote to assumptions and biases.

How to empathise

- I've included a great empathy tool in this book. If you want to turn straight away to Part 4 and apply it, go for it!
- Take the time to honestly consider someone's else's reality without the conscious and unconscious biases and assumptions you might normally apply. (I'm not having a dig here — we all have biases and assumptions. Turn back to chapter 9 if you need to think about yours a bit further.)
- Imagine what it would be like for you if someone who didn't know anything about you made decisions about your work, your personal life, the juxtaposition between the two. How would this make you feel? What would you want them to be careful about? Where would you want them to completely back off? Now this happens to all of us already thanks to laws and policies. However, we have a duty of care to go that extra step to make sure we are not putting anyone in harm's way, discriminating against them, ignoring them or making them jump through more hoops than anyone else.

Lens 3 — humanity

It's a big word, humanity; a big concept. Humanity is compassion, caring and consideration. When I think about the importance of humanity in relation to policy, it obliges me to ask:

- Who will suffer from a policy?
- Who will miss out from a policy?
- Who will be treated differently by a policy?
- How can we improve or protect equity for everyone?

The above are powerful questions, and I know you can think of more. Make sure you ask them. Make sure you consider humanity in every policy you work on — it's not a bargaining chip.

How to be humane

If you are a public servant, you represent the government of the day. In most interactions with government, there is a balance of power in favour of government. Assuming a superiority over those outside of government, for example, all the people with whom we need to engage to develop policy, is a slippery slope. Remember, if you are a public servant, you are exactly that: you serve the public, and humanity is at the heart of what you do.

In each of your interactions, be:

- respectful
- kind
- caring
- considerate
- compassionate
- sensitive
- honest
- responsible.

Lens 4 — flat and factual / frank and fearless / truth to power

Flat and factual, frank and fearless, and truth to power all 'talk' to the same principle, with slight nuances. We provide advice that is flat and factual, which means our advice is evidence-informed. Frank and fearless is how we provide the advice, and truth to power is the courage we sometimes need to get us over the frank and fearless line. Let's explore these a bit further.

The principle is that when we provide policy advice, we don't taper it to suit the desires of our audience. The principle ensures that our policy advice is always informed by triangulated evidence (multiple sources of evidence), and that if there isn't a solid evidence base, we say so. Remember, our job is to provide stakeholders, including the authorising environment, with the information they need, not what they desire. Policy decision-making must never be informed by cherry-picked evidence.

No doubt there is a tension between doing this professionally and with ease, and being terrified of delivering advice that you know is not going to be welcomed. I have watched in awe when people did this with such confidence and aplomb — maybe their tummy was doing backflips, like mine, but you couldn't tell. Remember that your professionalism is on the line. Ultimately, you won't be rewarded or professionally respected for people-pleasing instead of ensuring facts and evidence are the only things on the table.

How to give advice that is flat and factual, frank and fearless, and that holds truth to power

- Do your job — build advice that is evidence-informed.

- To do your job, you need to do your policy homework. Gather evidence; analyse evidence, including conflicting evidence; synthesise evidence; present evidence, warts and all.

- The public, your employers, the hierarchy are expecting you to do your job. They do not want you to provide uninformed opinion or to cherry-pick evidence to suit your audiences' desires (you know this already). Now, if a decision maker directs you to only provide the evidence that supports their position, you have some decision making of your own to do. I have been in that position. Document everything, and decide 1) if the decision maker's position is lawful, and if not, what you are going to do about it, and 2) whether you're in the right job. I wasn't.

- No doubt this can be excruciatingly tough at times. But I have confidence that you can do it — you're building your career as a *bloody good* policy officer.

Lens 5 — rigour

We must be thorough with all our policy efforts. We must, in the time available to us, turn over every possible stone. We must always be on the lookout for opportunities and risks. We must ponder all the 'what ifs'. We must consider and analyse the evidence we have. When we are rigorous, we build an environment of trust. We build an environment that creates *bloody good* policy work.

How to be rigorous

- Dot your I's and cross your T's.
- When you don't know something, say it.
- Test and stress test your work, and help your colleagues do the same with theirs.

- Seek assistance from colleagues. Find someone who knows how to do the things you don't. Sure, be willing to try, though don't fly by the seat of your pants — the consequences can be enormous.
- Seek feedback. Constructive criticism is a precious and valuable thing, so ask for it.
- Informed rigour is not the same as assumed confidence. Apply flat and factual, frank and fearless and truth to power all the time.

Lens 6 — practical and pragmatic

All of our policy advice must be achievable, realistic and reasonable. We can test and stress test whether our policies meet the practical and pragmatic yardsticks by:

- working with implementers
- seeking input from a diverse array of stakeholders, including those with lived experience
- calculating returns on investment, including social and environmental returns
- understanding, controlling and mitigating for risk
- ensuring financial viability
- establishing a framework for review, monitoring and evaluation from the get-go
- checking and double checking.

How to be practical and pragmatic

The above dot point list captures nicely the 'how to be practical and pragmatic'. In addition, I suggest you go back to chapter 8 and have a look at Griff's list of questions. In Part 4, we are also going to have a look at design thinking, which asks four key questions that relate to being practical and pragmatic:

1. Can 'it' be done?
2. Can we do 'it'?
3. Can they do 'it'?
4. How will we know?

Lens 7 — courage

When I think of courage, I usually think of people skydiving, abseiling or giving up all their worldly possessions to live off-grid. Though let me tell you something: it takes courage to be a *bloody good* policy officer. Just by the nature of government, we will often find ourselves walking (uphill) to the beat of someone else's drum. We need to know how to talk to people about difficult things, sensitive things, tragic and horrific things, and we don't always have formal training on this. At times we must manage unsolicited, unwanted, angry responses to our advice. At other times we must be the messenger of bad news. And often, we really are the meat in the sandwich — the people between the government of the day and the public.

Though there is another side to our courage. We have the courage to make a difference. We have the courage to do the hard yards, to lay the groundwork for those who will follow after us. We have the courage to have difficult discussions and to identify possible pathways and solutions. We have the courage to speak truth to power, to be flat and factual, to be frank and fearless. We have the courage to be honest, accountable and transparent. We are extraordinarily courageous.

How to be courageous

- Take your seven policy lenses with you wherever you go.
- Give yourself a break and be kind to yourself.

- Celebrate successes but also prepare for failures, and acknowledge and learn from them.
- Support your colleagues and make sure you get support when you need it.
- Keep on learning and growing.
- Be honest and truthful.
- If there is anything in this chapter that doesn't ring true to you or is not right for you, walk away from policy. If you're getting excited, keep going.

Takeaways

- Stay focussed on the people who will be impacted by a policy or its absence. You are doing policy work for them.
- *Bloody good* policy officers regularly use their metaphorical phoropter to look at policy through the lenses of curiosity, empathy, humanity, flat and factual / frank and fearless / truth to power, rigour, practical and pragmatic, and courage.

Action steps

- Keep your policy phoropter at the top of your policy kitbag. You will be using it all the time.
- Make the tips under each of the seven lenses part of your daily policy practice.
- Share the tips with your colleagues or team to build and measure your individual and collective experience of each of the lenses.

Part 4:

How to do *bloody* good policy work

"Dadirri — [the] inner, deep listening and quiet, still awareness".
Dr Miriam-Rose Ungunmerr Baumann AM, Inner Deep Listening
and Quiet Still Awareness, Miriam Rose Foundation

Part 4 is all about *doing* policy. I'll be filling your policy kitbag with tools I've used countless times, so I know they work. These policy tools will help you answer that recurring (perhaps sweaty hands, nauseous, I-want-to-hide) question — *what am I supposed to do now?*

The policy tools I'm sharing with you were not all specifically designed for policy; I am being cheeky in calling them policy tools. The tools were developed by business and education consultants, philosophers, academics, cognitive and climate scientists, for-purpose organisations, government departments and a strategy consultant. The policy tools have been used, reworked and reframed across multiple sectors and scenarios to better understand an opportunity or a problem; to explore the known, what we think we know and the unknown; to identify what can be influenced and what can't; to test hypotheses and to create solutions.

The nine policy tools, divided under three groups are:

1. Policy tools to craft the *now*
   - logic tree
   - policy ecosystem mapping
   - storylining
2. Policy tools to craft *what good looks like*
   - design thinking
   - PPESCTLE
   - solution deconstruction
3. Policy tools to craft the *change*
   - stakeholder engagement
   - empathy mapping
   - navigating complexity.

The layout of each policy tool follows the below format:

- an introduction to the policy tool, who developed it and why
- how the tool is valuable for policy development (some require more detail than others)
- some will have a policy scenario for you to consider
- a big nudge for you to have a go with the tool — either using the provided scenario, or for a policy you are working on or one that interests you.

Policy tools and stakeholders

Doing *bloody good* policy work comes from working with multiple stakeholders who have different understandings, experiences and motivations. Each time you use the policy tools, I want you to ask yourself how you can use that tool with stakeholders to always:

- build a deeper understanding of the policy you're developing
- identify barriers, opportunities and gaps
- test and stress test the practicality of solutions
- collate, analyse and synthesise evidence-informed data
- develop a policy that is definable, valuable, measurable and implementable
- understand your policy's impact on people.

You need to invite stakeholders to pull apart and critique your understanding of why a policy is needed, what it will do and how, what value it will create and whether proposed solutions are implementable. There is an inherent tension between a policy team and its stakeholders. Not all stakeholders' advice or positions will end up in a final policy. All stakeholders' advice, however, should be considered, acknowledged and respected. The policy tools provide a defendable process to manage this.

The alternative? Stakeholders will critique the policy when it is released, and you will learn publicly the 100+ ways your team didn't hit the mark. There are occasions when policies are developed without broad stakeholder engagement, such as the roll-out of the mandatory Covid-19 vaccinations. This is manageable to a point, but decision makers need to be prepared, and you might need to assist with that preparation in case of any fallout.

You can also use the outputs of your policy tools as a policy development's chronology. This is useful for three reasons. First, a chronology captures the start and end points of a policy's development, and everything that happens in between. Second, a chronology identifies policy decision-making points. Third, a chronology is a valuable source of data that can be measured and evaluated to inform future policy development.

Have fun with the policy tools. Play with them. Mix them up. Use them for different things — you don't have to use them for the same purpose as I suggest here. For example, in chapter 11, I use the logic tree to show how it can help you understand a policy commitment. It's also a very effective tool to better understand and test policy solutions.

Finally, don't be afraid to explore other tools and add them to your policy kitbag. Policy kitbags are quite magical as they always have room for more — more policy tools, more experiences (the good, the bad and the ugly), more chocolate, more insights, more policies… just *more*.

Enjoy, my policy friends, and let me know how you go.

Good luck!

Chapter 11

Policy tools to craft the now

The logic tree

The logic tree — aka the issue tree, the decision tree and the opportunity tree (the latter is what I like to call it) — was developed by McKinsey & Company[1] as a practical tool for breaking down and framing complex problems. At its most basic, the logic tree is a series of questions captured in a chart. Logic trees are fabulous tools to understand:

- *why* a policy is needed
- *what* a policy is intended to do
- *how* a policy will do 'it'
- *who* will do 'it' and whom 'it' will impact
- *when* a policy must be in place.

In this chapter we're going to look at how the logic tree is a great policy tool to understand *why* a policy is needed. By understanding the *why*, we will also understand the *now*. In the upcoming example, we are going to pull apart a policy commitment to understand the *now*. Interrogating a policy commitment is not debating whether it is the right policy or not — it's to understand *why* the decision makers want it, and from there, we can understand *how* to make the desired change happen.

Cautionary tale — if you start to feel the need to jump straight to solutions, definitely put the brakes on. You need to understand a policy commitment before you can start identifying solutions. I have to make a conscious effort to hit the policy solution brakes. A trick I use is to write down (what in my head are absolutely brilliant) policy solution ideas and park them. It's not a complete panacea — like any new habit, it takes time to bed down.

However, I have learnt, after practicing hasty-policy-solution-restraint for some time, that there are many benefits to putting the brakes on. The time you invest upfront in understanding a policy commitment and its *now* mitigates the significant risks of wasting time, money and resources, and causing unnecessary angst and frustration by going down the wrong path.

Applying the logic tree on a policy has two purposes. First, we must always understand correctly the policy commitment itself. If we don't, it's very difficult, in fact nigh on impossible, to work out *what good looks like*. And let's face it, an authorising environment's policy commitment is always the starting point of our work. Second, understanding a policy commitment helps us understand the *now* — what the current state of play is that the authorising environment has determined requires a change.

The logic tree will provide you an opportunity to think critically and objectively about the *now*. If you're ready to get started, throw your biases and assumptions into the bin, clear your head, heart and guts, and invite your team to do the same.

How do you start a logic tree? By highlighting all the words and/ or phrases in a policy commitment that need clarifying. Then ask questions about what you highlighted and use the logic tree as your template to capture all your questions. Write down everything that comes to mind. There are no right or wrong questions. You can go back and categorise, tidy up and remove duplications later.

The idea is to make an initial list of questions. Then go back to each question and break it down into more questions. Keep breaking each question down until you can't think of any new questions, or you reach saturation (that is, you keep asking the same or the same type of question).

Tips

Before we jump into an example logic tree, keep these tips in mind:

- The number of questions you will generate can be overwhelming — it's okay. It will settle.
- As with all the tools, you can use a logic tree to help you work through any part of a policy, for example, you could use a logic tree to test your solutions.
- It's very beneficial to collaborate on a logic tree with your stakeholders. It encourages understanding, creates opportunities for different perspectives to be considered, and will help create a shared narrative and language.
- Creating a logic tree with stakeholders will also quickly identify where there are similar and differing thoughts/questions as well as any outliers. Outliers are marvellous — they can open the most unexpected opportunities.

The logic tree in action

Let's have a go at starting a logic tree using one of The Australian Greens' 2022 Election Platform policy initiatives as an example. I'm going to do four things to demonstrate how a logic tree works:

1. list the words or phrases I need to clarify
2. ask a series of questions for three words/phrases from my list (you would do this for your entire list)
3. group my questions
4. identify where I can get answers to my questions.

Policy commitment: The Greens plan to "wipe student debt and ensure everyone can access a free, world-class education from early childhood, through to school to TAFE and Uni".[2,3]

Step 1: Identify the words and/or phrases that need clarification as there may be multiple interpretations. For me, it's —

- wipe student debt
- student
- ensure
- everyone
- access
- free
- world-class education
- early childhood
- school
- TAFE
- Uni.

Did you notice how it's nearly every word in the sentence? This is another reason why it's so important to pull apart the policy commitment upfront rather than risk later debates between people who have interpreted the same words and phrases (let alone the whole commitment) in different ways.

Step 2: Which questions, if answered critically, would provide the necessary clarity? For the purpose of this exercise, I chose only three words and phrases from my above list to demonstrate how this works. As I write the questions, I keep thinking of more questions that I could add to the logic tree (I won't, though, as it would make this a very long chapter!).

Words/phrases	Question 1	Question 2	Question 3	Question 4
Wipe student debt	What does wipe mean?	Will there be any means of testing?	Previous, existing and future debt?	Will refunds/subsidies be capped?
	Why is student debt a problem?	How do we know student debt is a problem?	How do uni, TAFE, and early childhood debt differ?	What is the average individual debt?
	What is the total student debt?	How will education be funded?	What is the debt per jurisdiction?	How does the debt differ between education types/courses/degrees?
World-class education (WCE)	What is WCE?	What is the demand for WCE?	How do we know WCE achieves better results?	What is the difference between WCE results and what we have now?
	What resources are needed for WCE?	Do educators, trainers and lecturers need to be retrained to provide WCE?	Does infrastructure need to be updated/replaced to meet WCE requirements?	Are the differences demonstrated across all subjects and learning types?
	What are the implementation costs for WCE?	What are the transition costs for the current models to WCE?	What is the estimated return on investment for WCE?	How significant are the differences between WCE and what we have now — will the return on investment be worthwhile?
Everyone	Who is everyone?	Does this include former, current and future students?	Will mature-age and international students be eligible?	Will private schools have to change their curricula?

The magic of the logic tree is that it naturally prompts us to ask more questions. And remember, keep breaking each question down until you can't think of any new questions, or you reach saturation.

The below table captures my questions about 'wipe student debt', 'world-class education', and 'everyone'.

Step 3: Group the above questions. Remember, the purpose for using the logic tree in this chapter is to understand *why* this policy is wanted and therefore to understand the *now*. The definition of policy is "a change that takes people (or people and things) from where they are now to where an organisation or a government wants them to be" (refer to chapter 1). I have grouped my questions as per the three policy components — *the now* (■), *the what good looks like* (★), *and the change* in the middle (🔄) — as illustrated in the below table. However, we will continue to focus on the *now*.

Straight away, we are able to differentiate between the *now*, the *change* and *what good looks like*, and there are a few outlier questions I'm not sure where to put right now. You'll also notice some questions have more than one symbol. That tells me I need to break these questions up to drill down further. I can also see that I need to ask more questions (for my entire word/phrase list) to better understand the *now*.

Words/phrases	Question 1	Question 2	Question 3	Question 4
Wipe student debt	What does wipe mean?	Will there be any means of testing?	■ Previous, existing and future debt?	Will refunds/subsidies be capped?
	■ Why is student debt a problem?	■ How do we know it is a problem?	■ How do uni, TAFE and early childhood debt differ?	■ What is the average individual debt?
	■ What is the total student debt?	How will education be funded?	■ What is the debt per jurisdiction?	■ How does the debt differ between education types/courses/degrees?
	What is WCE?	■ What is the demand for WCE?	★ Do we know WCE achieves better results?	■ What is the difference between WCE results and what we have now?
World-class education (WCE)	What resources are needed for WCE?	Do educators, trainers and lecturers need to be retrained in WCE?	Does infrastructure need to be updated/replaced to meet WCE requirements?	■ Are the differences demonstrated across all subjects and learning types?
	What are the implementation costs for WCE?	What are the transition costs for the current models to WCE?	★ What is the estimated return on investment for WCE?	■ How significant are the differences between WCE and what we have now — will the return on investment be worthwhile?
Everyone	■ Who is everyone?	Does this include former, current and future students?	★ Will mature age and international students be eligible?	Will private schools have to change their curricula?

Step 4: When you have asked all the questions you can think of and then grouped them, it's time to start thinking about where you can find the answers. The below list is a good start:

- The Australian Greens' Election 2020 manifesto[4]
- Desktop research, for example, to identify student debt data, jurisdictional comparisons, WCE and its comparison to what Australian curricula offers
- Informed discussion with your colleagues/superior. This doesn't mean hitting them up with a long list of questions but rather highlighting those areas you haven't been able to answer, or where you may have found supporting and/or different evidence. Always do your homework first.

What you, your team and supervisor identify may prompt a discussion with the decision maker(s) regarding a potential rewording of the commitment. I'm not suggesting you do this every time because it might not be necessary. However, from the very early stages of the logic tree above, I wonder whether the commitment needs to be tightened, for example, *by 2030 all students commencing university will benefit from...* It is too soon for me to jump to any conclusions, though you can see by the handful of questions I've asked, that it's possible — and I say this with all due respect — that the commitment is too broad. The commitment could be better positioned to be definable, valuable, measurable and implementable. But I'm jumping way ahead here, and this is a discussion for senior staff to manage.

Your turn — logic tree activity

Create a logic tree to understand the *now* for a policy you have on your desk today. Identify where you can source answers to your questions and examine those questions for which you will need to seek clarity and/or further information. It would be fabulous to get your colleagues and stakeholders involved in this activity. See where it takes it you. It will be worth it.

Policy ecosystem mapping

If you have ever drawn a mind map, scribbled on a whiteboard or been part of a brainstorming session, you will quickly work out what a policy ecosystem mapping session is! Policy ecosystem mapping is my fancy way of saying mind mapping. Mind mapping is attributed to Tony Buzan,[5] an English author who popularised mental literacy. Mind maps have also been linked to the Porphyrian Tree created by 3rd century philosopher Porphyry of Tyre[6] to logically classify substances.

I use the concept of mind mapping to create policy ecosystem maps for each policy I work on — at the very beginning of the policy work and throughout policy development. Policy ecosystem mapping is an easy and effective way to identify:

- *who* will be the likely stakeholders
- *what* we know and don't know about budgets, resources, timeframes
- *what* we know and don't know about the policy commitment
- *what* the key high components of the policy are likely to be
- *what* existing policies and legislation may impact the policy we are working on or vice versa
- *what* are the opportunities, challenges, obstacles
- *who* are the main influencers
- *who* is likely going to be part of the authorising environment
- *whom* the policy will impact.

The above list is not exhaustive, though it's a solid start to understanding the *now*. The trick is to put a time limit on a policy ecosystem mapping session; I recommend 45 minutes maximum and see where you get to. Following an initial high-level policy ecosystem mapping session and the work it generates, you will identify opportunities to map other policy ecosystems that will further clarify the *now*. For example, you may dedicate 45 minutes to mapping the organisations that currently provide particular services, or to mapping the demographics of who the policy will be impacting, including where they are located — urban, regional, remote and/or very remote parts of Australia.

Policy ecosystem mapping requires five simple ingredients:

1. People — minimum one, maximum 16. It's better to do several policy ecosystem mapping sessions with smaller groups than trying to get a large group as it becomes too unwieldy.
2. Space to write. Two huge whiteboards are my preference — though you can certainly improvise for an online meeting, and there are also many mind map apps available to use.
3. Whiteboard markers (or your writing tool of choice) in several colours.
4. Energy.
5. Curiosity.

It's important to have a focal point for each policy ecosystem map. For the purposes of our activity, we are going to focus on understanding the *now*. As the policy development evolves, you will be able to drill down and focus on specific areas.

How to be a *bloody good* policy officer

I have five rules for policy ecosystem mapping:

1. Everybody's ideas are welcome — no idea can be left off the board.
2. Have somewhere to capture any early desires to jump straight to solutions and then get straight back to mapping.
3. Go quickly, keep the conversation alive, prompt each other to think of something else, don't get bogged down in the details. A full and messy board is a great result for a policy ecosystem map.
4. Invite different stakeholder groups, or a mixed stakeholder group, to do a policy ecosystem mapping session with you. Please make sure your stakeholders' engagement is not being swamped by an over-excited policy team! It's best when a policy team facilitates.
5. Do as many policy ecosystem maps as needed throughout a policy's development. I find policy ecosystem maps particularly useful to:
    ○ come back to for a check-in
    ○ drill down into different parts of a policy
    ○ divvy up tasks across a policy team.

My process for policy ecosystem mapping is as follows:

- Give one person the markers and whiteboard-noting responsibility.
- Give the same person permission to keep prompting the group (*What else?*) and to keep the group focussed (*We don't need details now, let's move on*, or *Interesting solution — let's park it*).
- Capture as much as you can in each session.
- When you've reached the 45-minute cap, or the group has naturally run out of things to add, take time to consider

what's on the board.

- Start to make groups of like comments with different colours. You might also draw links between groups as there could be conflicting points or counterpoints on the board.
- You could take it a step further and try to identify any areas that influence others.
- Decide what you are going to do next by assigning tasks and responsibilities.

Policy ecosystem mapping in action

I'm going to create a scenario from one of the overarching governance principles and supporting principles of the *Local Government Act 2020* (Vic)[7] that states:

"9(1) A Council must in the performance of its role give effect to the overarching governance principles"… one of which is

—

"9(2)(c) the economic, social and environmental sustainability of the municipal district including mitigation and planning for climate change risks, is to be promoted".

Here is my imaginary scenario:

- You are a new policy officer in a local council.
- Your policy team has been asked to prepare advice for the next council meeting as to what your local council needs to do to meet the legislative requirements for mitigating and planning for climate change risks in your municipality.
- Nobody in your team, including your team leader, has any experience in climate change mitigation and planning.
- Your team leader suggests you do a policy ecosystem mapping session to start to understand the now for your municipality. Your team created the below map in 45 minutes.

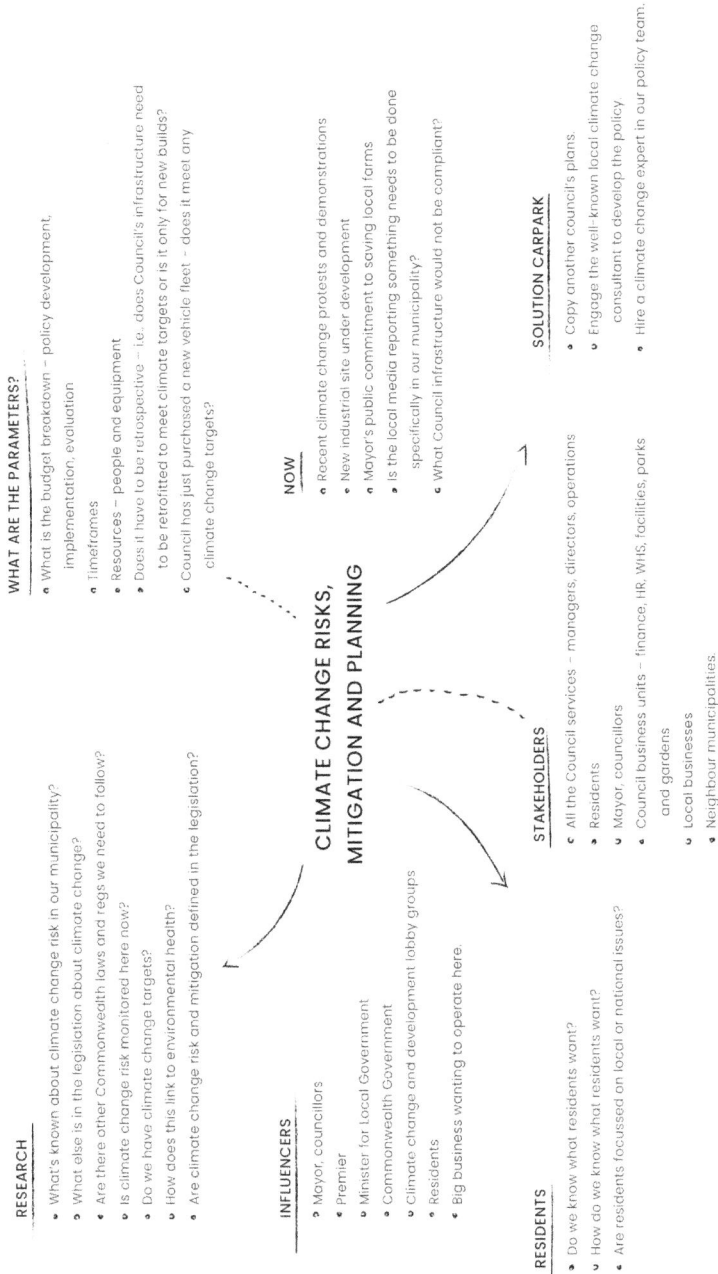

RESEARCH

- What's known about climate change risk in our municipality?
- What else is in the legislation about climate change?
- Are there other Commonwealth laws and regs we need to follow?
- Is climate change risk monitored here now?
- Do we have climate change targets?
- How does this link to environmental health?
- Are climate change risk and mitigation defined in the legislation?

INFLUENCERS

- Mayor, councillors
- Premier
- Minister for Local Government
- Commonwealth Government
- Climate change and development lobby groups
- Residents
- Big business wanting to operate here.

RESIDENTS

- Do we know what residents want?
- How do we know what residents want?
- Are residents focussed on local or national issues?

WHAT ARE THE PARAMETERS?

- What is the budget breakdown – policy development, implementation, evaluation
- Timeframes
- Resources – people and equipment
- Does it have to be retrospective – i.e. does Council's infrastructure need to be retrofitted to meet climate targets or is it only for new builds?
- Council has just purchased a new vehicle fleet – does it meet any climate change targets?

NOW

- Recent climate change protests and demonstrations
- New industrial site under development
- Mayor's public commitment to saving local farms
- Is the local media reporting something needs to be done specifically in our municipality?
- What Council infrastructure would not be compliant?

CLIMATE CHANGE RISKS, MITIGATION AND PLANNING

STAKEHOLDERS

- All the Council services – managers, directors, operations
- Residents
- Mayor, councillors
- Council business units – finance, HR, WHS, facilities, parks and gardens
- Local businesses
- Neighbour municipalities

SOLUTION CARPARK

- Copy another council's plans.
- Engage the well-known local climate change consultant to develop the policy
- Hire a climate change expert in our policy team.

Your turn — policy ecosystem mapping activity

I have three tasks for you:

- First, create a policy ecosystem map on your own for a policy that is on your desk now.
- Second, suggest to your team leader that the team does a policy ecosystem mapping session to understand the *now*.
- Third, discuss with your team when would be a good time to engage your stakeholders in a policy ecosystem mapping session to understand their experience and expertise of the *now*.

For all three tasks, be clear about the focus for that particular policy ecosystem mapping session. Focus on gaining an understanding of the policy commitment, or you might focus on a particular issue or opportunity. My preference is for you to build policy ecosystem mapping into your regular policy practice.

Always put the timer on, as it will force you to focus on the task at hand. It's also comforting for all participants to know there is a defined 'end', that the policy ecosystem mapping session is not going to be laboured for hours and hours. We've all been in meetings that have gone on for too long, and we know it is not productive, effective or efficient.

Finally, for the stakeholder policy ecosystem mapping session, make sure the stakeholders 'have the floor' for the majority of the session. You will learn so much, and it provides your stakeholders a simple way to share their knowledge, expertise and experience with your policy team.

PPESCTLE

In 1964, Harvard Business School Professor and author Francis J. Aguilar created a model to better understand business environments.[8, 9] The original version of his model was known as ETPS and had four components — economic, technical, political and social. After a couple of acronym changes, it became known as PESTLE or sometimes PESTEL, adding legal and environmental to the original model's components. PESTLE is a simple tool that helps us gain a deeper understanding about a policy by prompting us to analyse a policy from different perspectives.

In my work with a Commonwealth Government department, I was impressed to see that they had added an extra P (for people!) to their PESTLE model. That gave me the courage to add a C (for culture) to my version of the model — hence the tool we are going to explore next is PPESCTLE. Often the tool is presented as a table, however, I like it presented as a 'pie' as it immediately signals the importance of taking a holistic approach to our work.

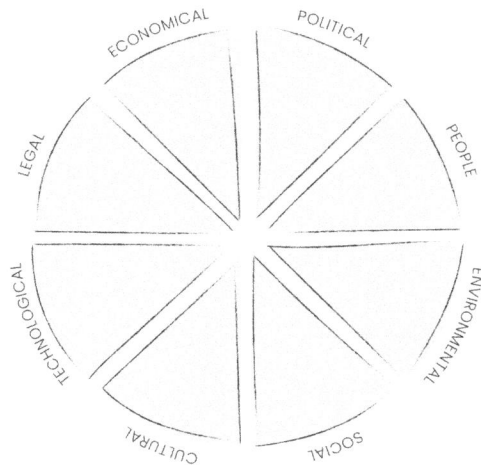

Source: adapted from toolshero[10]

The basic steps for 'doing' a PPESCTLE are as follows.

1. Always start with defining what each pie slice means with your stakeholder group. This will make sure there is a shared understanding of definitions, and it will reduce the risk of working at cross-purposes.

2. When using PPESCTLE with multiple stakeholder groups on the same issue, it's worthwhile to share the previous group's definitions with each new/subsequent group. Often you will find that there is agreement to continue with the same definitions (this can be useful when you get to analysing and synthesising). Occasionally, there will be differences — some subtle, some significant, and that's okay.

3. Choose any slice of the PPESCTLE pie to start. Definitely no rules here, nor is there a need to go clockwise or anti-clockwise — random choice is just fine.

4. You may find that there are one or more slices of pie you don't know anything about. In that case, make a note of these and make sure to take the time to do the necessary research to develop an informed-evidence base; then come back and fill in the pie.

5. There are multiple purposes for which to use a PPESCTLE. The way I regularly use it is to capture what I know from evidence-informed data, to identify what I don't know, and to identify from where or whom I can source the missing information. And this is exactly what you are going to do in your next activity.

Your turn — PPESCTLE activity

Scenario: you have recently commenced as a policy officer with one of the central Western Australian public service departments. You have been asked to draft a ministerial brief for noting to provide an update on Exmouth Gulf. Before you begin, let me quickly explain two things.

First, a central department or agency usually refers to the first minister's department, the treasury department and the attorney-general's department. These three departments represent the most senior and influential ministers of a government's cabinet.

Second, a ministerial brief *for noting* does not provide recommendations for decision making, rather, it provides advice on a particular issue to keep the minister informed, for example, an update on the progress of a policy or the outcomes of a strategic meeting. A signed copy of the ministerial brief will be returned to your department. Sometimes a minister may seek clarity on your advice, ask for further information, or request further action. There are processes that need to be followed if a minister requests anything further, and you will need to check with your supervisor as to what you need to do next. In some cases, the minister won't sign the brief, in which case you should definitely check with your supervisor about your next steps.

Back to our scenario. Your minister requires information as to the current state of play (the *now*) of three key policy influencers, namely:

- Gascoyne Gateway Ltd, that wishes to develop an industrial port at Qualing Pool in the Exmouth Gulf.[11]
- Protect Ningaloo, a grassroots initiative, that opposes the proposed Gascoyne Gateway Ltd development.[12]
- The Exmouth Gulf Taskforce that was established by the WA Minister for Energy; Environment; Climate Action to provide high-level advice to the Minister on social, cultural and environmental management of the Exmouth Gulf and its surrounds.[13]

Before you get stuck in, I need you to do a small piece of preparation and write down your assumptions and biases about the three above policy influencers to ensure that your assumptions and biases do not distort your advice.

Staying neutral is not easy, particularly in this activity's example. You may have a steadfast position to support the industrial port, or perhaps you have an unwavering commitment to save the reef. Perhaps you don't know anything about the taskforce.

However, maintaining neutrality is important for many reasons though I will highlight just two. One, your credibility and professionalism will be shot to pieces if you can't be trusted to provide flat and factual advice. Two, you will lose a critical opportunity to build a deep understanding of all the issues and opportunities that are at stake. This loss will directly impact the advice you prepare and could ultimately bear consequences for the people and things that will be impacted by whatever the authorising environment does with your advice.

Now that you have noted your assumptions and biases, you are ready to start a PPESCTLE. Complete a PPESCTLE for each of the policy influencers by following the five steps on p. 140. Feel free to gather your information in a different format — I concede that trying to fill in a pie chart is not practical! You are going to capture:

- What you know (evidence-informed) about each of the policy influencers' positions *now* on the proposed development
- What questions you need answered about each of the policy influencers' positions *now* on the proposed development
- From whom or from where you can get answers to your questions.

You will be able to:

- create an informed picture through the PPESCTLE activity of what the *now* looks and feels like for the three policy influencers' perspectives and positions
- identify if a particular issue(s) is more prominent than others, this might indicate, for example, that resolution needs to be found for it before any further action
- identify if there are areas of agreement or similar approaches
- identify risks and challenges for which you may also have gathered insights from the policy influencers as to possible solutions
- prepare a comprehensive, flat and factual brief for noting — congratulations!

Chapter 12

Policy tools to craft what good looks like

Design thinking

Design was first considered as a way of thinking in the late 1960s by Herbert A Simon, a cognitive scientist and Nobel Prize laureate.[1, 2] From the 60s, when it mainly featured in architecture and engineering practices, design thinking has evolved to become the model for innovative pursuits for multiple professional practices, including that of policy. Using design thinking as part of your policy development will:

- increase collaboration (working with all the people who should be involved)
- increase co-design (working with others to define problems, shape solutions, and then test and stress test them)
- increase your evidence base with relevant and contemporary information
- increase trust between you, your team and your stakeholders
- enhance the authorising environment's decision making
- reduce risks of a policy not achieving the desired goals
- create pragmatic and practical solutions that puts your policy right on the path to *what good looks like.*

The below illustration shows the conceptualisation of design thinking — a user-centric, five-pronged innovation and ideation process underpinned by empathy, collaboration and experimentation in the pursuit of innovative solutions as opposed to focusing on problems.

144

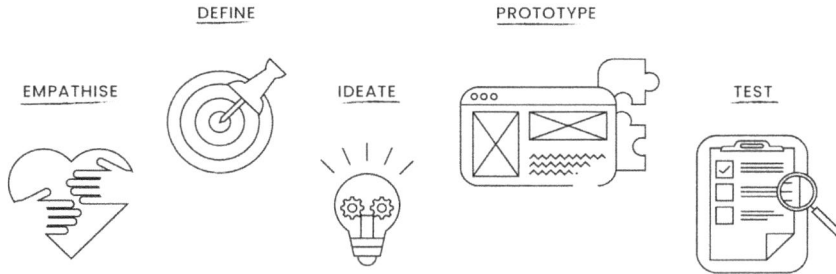

Design thinking is flexible, responsive, unconstrained and agile, so it can sit comfortably within our policy practice, however, it may not be an obvious or easy path for public servants.

Over the years I have seen, heard and been part of policy pursuits guided by flexibility, responsiveness, creativity and agility. Nevertheless, the system in which you work (refer to chapters 4 and 5) is structured, contained, at times frustratingly obtuse and unmalleable, and not always open to a design thinking approach. That said, I firmly believe that just because something is difficult to implement or takes time to see results, if it leads to *what good looks like*, it must be part of our policy kitbag.

Often in policy we are faced with extraordinarily complex, complicated and intractable problems. These types of policy problems — collectively called wicked policy problems, a phrase coined by design theorists Horst Rittel and Melvin Rittel in the 1970s — are difficult to define and are embedded in complex social, environmental, cultural, political, structural and economic systems and contexts.[3]

With wicked policy problems, it is difficult if not impossible to define *what good looks like*. Consider for a moment any of the armed conflicts or humanitarian crises in the world today. Some of these have been raging for decades, even crossing from the 20th to the 21st century. While relief or peace may be achieved for periods of time, they can be difficult to maintain. Design thinking provides a framework to recognise the enormity of the wicked problems while encouraging us to keep going. While we may not be able to achieve the desired change, we are hopefully paving the path for those who will follow to take the next step towards *what good looks like*.

The application of design thinking is not limited to wicked policy problems. It can be used across an array of policy problems and opportunities, and that's exactly what we are going to do next. This time though, I am not going to provide you a full example of what 'doing' design thinking looks like. This time I'm going to take you through the process with some examples and then leave you to bring design thinking to life in your work. Let's start by considering the five design thinking steps — **empathise, define, ideate, prototype, test**.

Design thinking's human-centred approach ensures our focus is to **empathise** and understand those who are or will be impacted ('end users' is the term commonly found in design thinking, reflecting its genesis in architecture and engineering) by a policy or the absence of one. We are empathetic when we care about:

- how people will be impacted by a policy
- the people who won't be able to access a policy
- how implementing a policy impacts the people working on the frontline
- people, full stop.

From empathising with those who are or will be impacted by a policy, we can **define** a problem or an opportunity from the evidence we have gathered through our human-centred approach, not strictly from a system or structural perspective. For example:

- A cost-of-living policy may define the problem as 'families having less money for discretionary spending', or an informed definition of the problem may be 'single parents are sacrificing their own meals to feed their kids'.
- An emergency response policy may define a problem as 'disaster victims have lost everything', or an informed definition of the problem could be 'emergency services can't meet the needs of the disaster victims without help from the wider community'.

When we have defined the problem, we can start to **ideate**. Ideating is very much what you did with the policy ecosystem mapping, so you know what to do! Though don't stop at the whiteboards — role play, visualise the path of change, and craft stories about people's experiences to identify solutions from considering the problem as it has been articulated through your human-centred approach. The number one rule of policy ecosystem mapping applies — everybody's ideas are welcome, every solution must be captured. The purpose of ideating is to create as many solutions as possible. It's not about quality; even a beginning of an idea is important to capture. One other rule applies — assumptions and biases must be challenged.

After ideating, you will develop tangible **prototypes** for your solutions. The prototypes don't need to be fancy — they could be simple drawings, for example, the reduced number of steps to complete an online application form for a disability allowance versus a hard copy form. Develop a prototype for multiple solutions, not just one. If you unnecessarily put constraints on the process, you will lose the power of design thinking.

Now you are ready to **test** your solutions to actively seek feedback about your hypotheses. In the disability allowance application example, you would seek feedback from people including those who:

- have a disability
- need to make an application
- care for people with a disability
- process disability support applications
- manage the call centre and those who manage the face-to-face customer counter
- might need to build a new online application system for the application.

Each piece of their feedback will enhance your solutions to be better positioned to achieve the required change.

Your turn — design thinking

Get a group of your team members together and have a go at applying design thinking to a solution for a policy you are working on now. Work through the five design thinking steps — empathise, define, ideate, prototype, test. Most importantly, give yourselves permission to throw constraints and rules out the window, and enjoy what design thinking has to offer. Your policy work will be enhanced exponentially. Did I mention that you're going to test the solutions you just crafted in the next task?

Solution deconstruction

All the activities you have done so far have been focussed on pulling problems apart, or deconstructing them, to understand them better. Deconstruction is a solid approach to gain a deeper understanding of why a problem is a problem; what people, organisations and/or things are experiencing; and, as you experienced with the logic tree, to clearly understand the drivers behind a policy position.

Deconstructing our solutions is equally valuable — we must make sure they are going to achieve the desired change. Sometimes we (okay, I mean me) can get carried away with a solution and be blind to its flaws or gaps, or just blind to the reality that it is never going to work. It's not about playing Negative Nelly; it's about making sure our solutions are as watertight as possible to drive the desired change. Remember the last tip I gave you about implementation in chapter 2? I want you to apply this here — test for failure. It is a very powerful approach. Why? Because it's easier to see what we have developed (through a whole lot of effort) as being 'right'; if we force ourselves to look at our solutions more critically, they have a better chance of achieving *what good looks like*.

Deconstruction is a philosophical and critical theory approach developed by philosopher Jacques Derrida.[4] It is an approach to analysis that explicitly seeks to identify assumptions and contradictions. However, we're moving away from Derrida's application of the analysis of language and logic in philosophical and literary text.

We will use Derrida's deconstruction theory to analyse, test and stress test our policy solutions — hence solution deconstruction. I presume (fingers crossed) that you have one, maybe two solutions you developed as prototypes in the design thinking activity. You would have already tested your prototypes as part of that activity, but now you're going to test them even further.

There are different elements to deconstruct a solution, including though not limited to:

- Cost effectiveness — can the outcomes or benefits of a solution be achieved at the lowest possible cost?

- Practical to implement — is a solution 'doable'?
- Required inputs — are the people, infrastructure, technology and funding (and whatever else is required) available and accessible?
- Inter- and intra-dependencies — does a solution rely on another solution(s), or is a solution the outcome of something else?
- Contestability — is the solution the most effective, efficient and productive one?
- The do-nothing approach — what would be the consequences if a solution wasn't implemented?

Your turn — solution deconstruction

I want you to choose one of your solutions from the design thinking activity you did. Then you are going to switch hats from the designer to the dismantler and:

- Choose at least one type of solution deconstruction approach from the list above.
- Pull apart your solution. Question everything, for example —
  - what systems are required for the solution
  - whether existing technology meets the solution needs or if new/different technology is required
  - who will drive, implement and manage the solution
  - whether it is a known solution or if will it be rolled out as a pilot
  - whether the solution exists in another sector and if is it applicable
  - whether the solution is within available budget and earmarked for delivery.

Similarly to the logic tree in chapter 11, there is no right or wrong question. However, when deconstructing a solution, you need to be confident that you have satisfactorily tested and stress tested it. The best way to deconstruct your solution is to do it with the stakeholders who you anticipated will be involved at the development, implementation, 'receiving' and evaluation of your solution.

Don't hold off deconstructing your solutions; do it throughout policy development. You and your stakeholders will learn so much about your solutions and will be able to improve them every time. Though this can sometimes mean throwing a solution or two in the bin and starting again, better now than after implementation has failed.

Storylining

The tools in *Rollercoaster* create valuable insights and pathways to developing *bloody good* policy. They all require you to engage and communicate with other people and, more often than not, to prepare for other people to engage and communicate — your supervisor, your head of department, your minister.

Engagement and communication are important skills, though they can be really tricky. Sometimes it's the subject that's tough, such as advising the minister that things haven't gone to plan or informing your stakeholders that the work you have done together will be put on hold. At other times, it's not the subject but working out, for example, the best way to engage with a group of high-profile and influential stakeholders, or writing your very first brief. I remember the first time I had to write a cabinet submission. I'll tell it to you straight — I knew what I was writing about, but I had no idea how to start let alone finish a whole cabinet submission. It was one of those 'learn from your failure' moments for me! Storylining would have been very handy.

Scientists use storylining to first capture past events and plausible future events or pathways, then build a narrative of credible future climates to enhance risk awareness.[5] Storylining is also practicable for policy development as it helps you craft timely, meaningful and impactful communications to underpin your engagement with the public and with identified stakeholder groups. Davina Stanley and Gerard Castles cleverly capture in the title of their version of storylining, *The So What Strategy*,[6] the one outcome you must always mitigate — when your audience gets to the end (some may not even make it halfway) of your communication only to ask you, *So what?* Ouch — they don't know why you have communicated with them, and you're about to lose their attention if you haven't already.

Before we look at how you can use storylining, let's first look at two formal engagement models. The first is a government's public service engagement model (aka engagement framework or community engagement model); the second is how a government and its public service engage with each other. Understanding when and why you would use different types of engagement will inform the development of your storyline.

Government / public service engagement models

Most governments and their public service will have an engagement model. Sometimes individual departments will have a specific engagement model relevant to their portfolio(s), for example, health departments may have a public health engagement model. The purpose of engagement models is to establish how a government and its public service will involve its citizens and specific stakeholder groups to share information and to inform policy development, even policy decision making. While created for governments and their public services, the model can be adjusted to suit organisations and businesses outside of government.

Typically, there are four to five types of engagement as illustrated below.

Inform	Consult	Involve	Collaborate	Empower
To provide stakeholders timely and relevant information, without inviting them to respond. **Inform** is 'one-way' communication. Example: advising residents of localised water contamination and where they can access potable water.	To seek information and feedback from our stakeholders to inform policy development. **Consult** is 'two-way' communication focussed on gathering answers to questions. Example: changing public school term dates.	To work directly with stakeholders throughout policy development to ensure issues, concerns and opportunities are understood and considered. **Involve** is 'two- or multi-way' communication where learning takes place for all stakeholders including 'us'. Example: establishing a neighbourhood syringe exchange program.	To partner with stakeholders and/or stakeholder groups for the development of mutually agreed solutions and joint plans of action best suited to achieve desired policy outputs and outcomes. **Collaborate** is 'multi-way' communication where all those involved benefit from learning, negotiation and decision making to work together to drive change. Example: the National Agreement on Closing the Gap[7] including the establishment of the Joint Council on Closing the Gap.	To delegate decision making to stakeholders on a particular issue. Stakeholders are enabled and equipped to actively contribute to the achievement of outputs and outcomes. **Empower** is a 'multi-way' communication focussed on transitioning decision making from government to an external party. Example: Transition of health services to Aboriginal Community Controlled Health Organisations.

Our stakeholder commitment:	Our stakeholder commitment:	Our stakeholder commitment:	Our stakeholder commitment:	Our stakeholder commitment:
We will keep you informed.	We will seek your expertise and experience on matters that are important to you to inform policy development. We will share information with you regularly. At times we may seek further advice from you ('two-way' communication), at other times we will provide you progress updates ('one-way' communication).	We will work with you so that the issues, concerns and opportunities you identify inform and may also be reflected in policy solutions ('two-way' communication). We will advise you as to how your input influenced our policy solution(s) ('one-way' communication).	We recognise and respect your experience and expertise. We will work with you to agree on what we will implement, and we will incorporate your advice and recommendations into policy outputs and outcomes to the maximum extent possible.	We will support you to establish your governance, system and process frameworks. We will support and complement your actions where you require our support, for example, in cross-sector collaborations and involvement.
Inform in practice: Emergency information alerts Public health fact sheets Media releases, announcements, interviews.	**Consult in practice:** Public surveys Focus groups Public meetings.	**Involve in practice:** Cross-sector working groups Expert advisory panels.	**Collaborate in practice:** Joint projects and partnerships Joint action plan investment and delivery.	**Empower in practice:** Local decision making Progressing through consult, involve and collaborate.

How governments and their public services engage with each other

Governments and their public services have a formal engagement structure that underpins how they engage and communicate with each other. In chapter 6, I pointed out that there are different types of briefs that serve different engagement and communication needs. Your department will have its suite of brief templates that will be standardised across the public service. There are two things you need to pop on your to-do list now — one, make sure you know how to access the suite of brief templates and two, seek approval to do a ministerial writing course. (I wish I had done this before attempting my first cabinet submission!)

Storylining in practice

Whether you are engaging with the public and external stakeholders or whether you are communicating with a minister, you need to prepare. Enter storylining. A storyline builds a narrative relevant to those with whom you need to engage. To create a storyline, you need to know:

- *why* you need to communicate
- *what* needs to be communicated
- with *whom* you need to communicate
- *when* you need to communicate
- *what* will matter to the people with whom you are communicating *and* what you need from them.

The last dot point above is the clincher for successful storylining — to find the balance between satisfying the needs of your different audiences *and* obtaining what you need from them. Let's go back to the example we used in the above table to describe the inform engagement type — a government informing homeowners about a water contamination in their area. Both the homeowners and the government get what they need — homeowners know to stay away from contaminated water and where to get potable water *and* the government is meeting its obligation to protect the health of its citizens.

To build a storyline, you need evidence-based information. Though you likely won't use all the information in your engagement and communication, and this is the power of storylining. Let's go back again to the contaminated water. Would it be useful in the first instance for the government to share the comprehensive water testing results with the householders? Short answer — no. While water testing information will be shared, and it's important to understand that water testing has been completed, the most important message in this scenario is to inform householders that alternative sources of potable water are available to them.

Stanley and Castle's four tools to scope your communication (I've added a fifth one, engagement type, to the list) will help you develop the craft of storylining:

1. **Context** — what's the setting, what's happening?
2. **Trigger** — why is engagement/communication required 'now'?
3. **Question** — what is the most important question that needs to be answered for the people who are being engaged/communicated with?
4. **Focus** — what is the focus of the engagement/communication?
5. **Engagement type** — what is the type of engagement required if this relates to public and/or stakeholder engagement, or what type of brief is required if it's a department-to-government communication? And so that you know — you'll need a covering brief too, if you are

developing communication for a minister or department head to deliver or facilitate an engagement!

The below is an example of how to apply the above five elements based on a scenario of a government's response to people affected by a natural disaster.

Context: natural disaster recovery effort

Trigger: we need to inform community members affected by the recent flood/cyclone/bushfire/earthquake/tsunami of what to expect in the recovery effort

Question: is the information 'they' shared with me what I need right now?

Focus: to ensure all affected community members attend a town hall meeting that will tell them how to access recovery effort support

Engagement type: inform, to provide affected community members with timely and relevant information.

Let's now zoom out to consider the evidence that would need to be collated to inform the above engagement. Please note this example has been prepared purely for the purposes of this activity — I am not a natural disaster recovery expert.

Evidence:

Temporary emergency accommodation options	Food, drinking water, clothing and personal supplies	Medical triage, supplies and emergencies
Affected community members need to choose one of the below options. • Option 1: Remain in the provided emergency shelter. • Option 2: Remain outside the emergency declared area. There will be a continued presence in the emergency shelter for each individual or family group to: • Confirm their accommodation preference • Provide contact details including next of kin.	The below products will be provided at the emergency shelter facility. • Food and drinking water will be provided daily at the emergency shelter by [provider] • Clothing will be provided weekly by [provider], noting there will be a set number of items per individual. • Personal supplies will be provided by [provider], weekly. Community members not staying at the emergency shelter need to advise the recovery team if they require food.	• Onsite medical presence will be reduced to 3/week. • Medicines and supplies will be dispensed 3/week. • Medical emergencies will be managed by [provider]. • GPs and pharmacies in the neighbouring communities of [names] have prioritised bookings and services for victims of the disaster. • Appointments with a neighbouring GP will be available via the disaster recovery app.

Visiting support services	Clean-up status	Disaster recovery communication channels
The following services will be provided onsite: • Pastoral care • Local schools There will be a mix of town hall meetings plus individual meetings for pastoral care. Bookings for individual meetings will be available via the disaster recovery app. Victims of the disaster not staying at the shelter have full access to these services.	• Local services, the army and volunteers are continuing the clean-up which is expected to be completed by [date]. • People will be able to return to their properties based on a risk assessment at the conclusion of the clean-up. • Transport will be provided to return people to their properties. • Accommodation will remain available for those whose properties are declared uninhabitable.	The emergency recovery team will: • Provide daily updates via our app and on the emergency shelter notice boards. • Advise of any changes or updates in a timely manner. • Hold the next town hall meeting on [date]. • The next town hall meeting will hopefully be video streamed for those who have found accommodation with friends or family.
Further actions for the recovery team to consider What needs to be prepared for out-of-scope issues raised at the town hall meeting: insurance including Medicare (what will be covered), when they will be notified of the damage to their home, assets and pets/livestock (is there a vet checking on them?), suitable areas to practice different faiths, whether there will be a suspension of regular household bills (power, water etc.).		

Time to start crafting that first communication. Will you focus on all the information you have gathered, or getting affected community members to the town hall meeting? My suggestion — go for the latter. Getting people to the town hall meeting is the first step. Below is my first crack at drafting a communication to the affected community members.

Dear [community name] resident,

As part of our disaster recovery effort, we will be holding a community information meeting at the emergency centre on [date] [time]. We ask that you attend so that you can receive important information for you and your family.

At the meeting we will discuss:

- *Your temporary emergency accommodation options*
- *Provision of food, drinking water, clothing and personal items*
- *Medical triage, supplies and emergencies*
- *Visiting support services*
- *Clean-up status*
- *Disaster recovery effort team communication channels.*

We will check your names as you arrive so that we can follow up with those who haven't been able to attend.

Kindest regards,
The Disaster Recovery Team

Go back to pp. 158-159 to check that each item has been adequately addressed in my communication. If not, what would you change or add? The purpose of me asking you this question is to encourage you to do the same. Have at least one other team member review your work. You need to know 'now' if something is missing, incorrect, superfluous, or simply does not make sense. Ask yourself: *is this clear? Will it meet the community members' needs? Will it meet our needs?*

Before you jump in, keep in mind that you can use the storyline format for simple communications such as an email as well as for detailed, complex communications such as a cabinet submission.

Your turn — storylining activity

For your storylining activity, I want you to prepare a storyline using the five-step tool on p. 156 for each of the three communications below. You can base the communication on a policy you are working on right now or create a scenario for a policy that interests you.

1. an email from your supervisor to stakeholders inviting them to take part in a policy working group
2. introduction speaking points for your supervisor at the first stakeholder working group
3. a policy progress report for the minister (check which brief template will best suit this purpose)

I also have one more activity for you — actually, it's a little extra for your policy kitbag. I want you to consider how you will build trustworthiness through well informed and targeted engagements and communications. All you need to do is look at the Trust Equation©[8] and how it reflects your approach to your all your work — it's a very handy tool.

$$T = \frac{C + R + I}{S}$$

Trustworthiness = (Credibility + Reliability + Intimacy) / Self-Orientation

P.S. Remember to check out your department's brief suite and to sign up for a ministerial writing course.

Chapter 13

Policy tools to craft the change

Stakeholder engagement

Stakeholders and their engagement are mentioned countless times throughout *Rollercoaster*. By the time you get to the last page, you would have been prompted about a hundred times to think about stakeholders and their engagement. The point being, we can't develop policy without stakeholders.

In this chapter I will share with you Mendelow's power-interest matrix.[1] Aubrey Mendelow, a former Kent State University Professor of Management and Information Systems, analysed stakeholders by measuring and placing a value on their interest and power, which would determine their level of impact on business decisions. What captures my attention about Mendelow's matrix, along with work by other scholars in the 60s, is the insight that stakeholders "depend on an organization for the realization of some of their goals, and in turn, the organization depends on them in some way for the full realization of its goals".[2] This captures the essence of governments' (and other types of organisations') inter- and intra-dependent relationships with their stakeholders and vice versa when developing policy. It also aligns to storylining in the previous chapter — 'what' will matter to the people with whom you are communicating *and* what you need from them.

The influence-interest matrix

Let's focus first on the language of influence and interest. I have tweaked Mendelow's matrix, changing stakeholder *power* to stakeholder *influence*. There is one important reason for this. While individuals and organisations can and do wield power over government, in the main, there is usually an imbalance of power in favour of a government 'over' its stakeholders.

Some stakeholders will keenly feel the power imbalance in their relationship with government, reflecting their lived experience of government policy. Others will take a pragmatic approach and keep chipping away at influencing government policy making. And for many, it has been a beneficial relationship — so all is not lost. However, it is very important when working in policy to be conscious of the imbalance, particularly if you work in a public service, to make sure you don't inadvertently take advantage of it.

Influence refers to the ability of an individual, group of people or organisation(s) to sway an authorising environment's decision making, the policy development process and/or the wider community's response to a policy development.

Stakeholder interest is multi-faceted. Interest can be generated by a desire to see a policy 'get over the line'. It can also be the reverse, in which stakeholder interest would be to make sure a policy doesn't get even close to the line. Sometimes interest will be from the perspective that investment in one policy risks diluting the investment in another. At times policy development can find itself in the throes of a power negotiation — think of the interest-driven power plays in relation to climate change policy.

Now let's consider what we mean by stakeholders. Certainly, the definition of stakeholder being someone with a pecuniary interest in an organisation is still valid. The public at large and individual citizens also have a pecuniary interest in government policies, and they generally have an interest in how governments invest public funds. However, 'stakeholder' is used more widely now to encompass a far broader range of people with whom an organisation, a government department or a government wishes to engage. The below table is one way for you to strategically group stakeholders.

Stakeholder types[3]

Government & parliament decision makers	Policy teams	Public service decision makers	Public sector leaders
• Your minister • Other ministers, members of the opposition and independent members • Local government members • Cabinet and sub-committees of cabinet.	• Policy teams in your department, public service or from other jurisdictions within and outside of Australia.	• Your policy and department hierarchy • Policy governance committees.	• Public service leaders • Independent statutory officers • Executive / senior cross-department committees.
Public service expertise	**Experts outside of government**	**People with experience**	
• Public servants with expertise not available in your team, and maybe not in your department, i.e., lawyers, scientists, economists,	• Aboriginal Community Controlled Organisations • Peak bodies • Non-government organisations • For-purpose organisations	• People with lived experience • Community leaders • Community groups • Recipients of a government funded service	

Public service expertise	Experts outside of government	People with experience	
behavioural experts, medical experts, service delivery experts.	• Subject matter experts including academics • Private sector leaders • Industry and business leaders and or representative bodies.	• People who are or will be impacted by a policy, or its absence • The broader public.	

So, who could be considered a stakeholder for policy development? Short answer — pretty much anyone. However, rigour must be applied, including being absolutely clear as to why you would engage someone or an organisation as a stakeholder.

Remember that policy is not developed in a static environment. As such, stakeholders' influence and interest will be changed by what is going on around them and by whether or not they have the 'ear' of a minister or a government. An example would be a community leader who does not hold any influence, though who, following a change of government, may find the incoming government courting their opinion and advice. This is not uncommon across all types of stakeholders.

It's also not uncommon for stakeholders to flex their influence to ensure a policy platform or initiative is in their best interest; for example, trade unions, the Pharmacy Guild of Australia and Greenpeace are particularly active when a policy has implications for their sector. The sphere of interest is continually changing, and as such, it's important to keep your stakeholder influence-interest matrix up to date.

It's also important to be mindful of those with high interest and low influence — often those who will be directly impacted by a policy or by a policy's absence. These people are key stakeholders too, and you must actively seek to engage them in the policy development process. On the flip side, 'people power' can increase influence. Keep in mind, however, that not everyone will participate willingly, and some may refuse — once bitten, twice shy.

Let's now turn our minds to how the influence-interest matrix works. The matrix prompts us to classify stakeholders in one of the quadrants as illustrated below. It's important to clarify the purpose of why stakeholders would be engaged before placing them into the quadrants. It could be to:

- engage them in a policy development working group
- be part of an expert panel
- understand their lived experiences of a policy or lack of a policy
- or to keep them informed of a policy development.

Remember, the need to engage stakeholders may change over the course of a policy development. New or additional stakeholders may be identified. Sometimes only limited engagement is required. Some stakeholders may be invited to be part of a policy development co-design after being part of a focus group. Be purposeful, agile and flexible with the stakeholder engagement approach — and make sure you do your stakeholder homework.

Once the purpose of a stakeholder engagement is clarified, it's then possible to develop a stakeholder list. Stakeholder lists need to be specific, meaning individual organisations and individual people or roles need to be identified. Sometimes research and/or networking is required to get a list to a point where it's useful, and taking time to do this is a worthwhile investment.

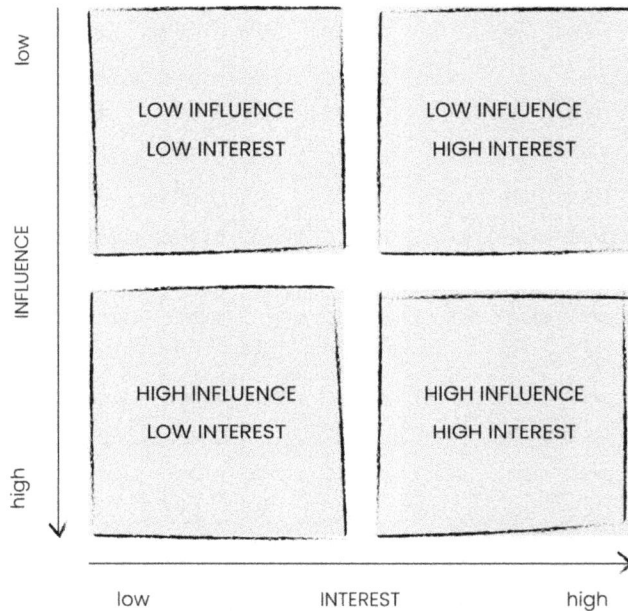

Source: adapted from boardmix[4]

Your turn — interest-influence matrix activity

For this activity I want you to choose a policy that you are working on or use a policy scenario from one of the other *Rollercoaster* activities, and do three things:

1. Clarify why you need to engage stakeholders and why they would accept to engage.
2. Make a stakeholder list, being as specific as possible. Where you're not sure, make a note of where or from whom you might be able to find the information. If you are doing this activity on an active policy development, complete this task

before moving to number three.

3. Consider which quadrant your stakeholders fit in. Usually you'll have stakeholders in each quadrant — it doesn't matter at this stage, just fill the matrix!

As with all the activities, this one is also beneficial to do in a group. If you are doing this for an active policy development, you need to get at least some of your team involved. Remember to go back occasionally to check whether a stakeholder's influence has changed or just to check that everyone is still where you had initially placed them.

Empathy mapping

Dave Gray, co-founder of XPlane strategy consultants,[5] developed empathy mapping. Empathy mapping, described as a powerful visualisation tool, helps people to use emotional intelligence (aka EQ) to gain insights into other people or organisations. Using empathy mapping will allow you to better understand the motivations of others, what is influencing them, what they most want to happen, what they most fear happening, what their day-to-day looks like.

The insights for policy development I have gained from empathy mapping include though are not limited to:

- How to best communicate with different stakeholders, for example, some may prefer detailed qualitative briefs, others only want to see visualisations of data (tables, graphs, heatmaps), some may prefer a face-to-face meeting before a brief is drafted
- Recognising how I can shape my work to meet the needs of stakeholders by understanding their motivations, aspirations

and fears

- Identifying who and what is influencing stakeholders, for example, what reputable data sources they are accessing and whether the data sources are the same or different to the ones I have researched

- Ensuring I research what I don't know. Not knowing a stakeholder well, even from a distance, doesn't invite us to barge in without doing our homework first.

It's valuable to empathy map the different people in your authorising environment. It's also valuable to empathy map organisations you may be partnering with or who may oppose the policy you are developing. Of course, empathy mapping those who will be impacted by a policy, or by a policy's absence, is highly beneficial to policy development. There's really no limit to who you can empathy map!

The seven key steps to empathy mapping are detailed below, to which I have added an additional step (number 2). Go through them and then jump straight to your next activity.

1. Identify who you are going to map and what is the purpose of mapping them.
2. Take the time to list your assumptions and biases about the person/organisation you chose as this will help balance your approach to mapping them.
3. Do your homework on the person/organisation before mapping them. It's quite possible you won't know the answers to every empathy map question. Do your best to find out what you can; for example, to get a feel for a new

minister, you could look up their media releases and their speeches on Hansard.*

4. Start your mapping with the questions under 'See'.
5. Work your way clockwise around the outer parts of the map. If you are doing an empathy map with your team, you can work through all the questions together or divvy them up.
6. Once you have finished answering all the questions on the outside of the map, go to the questions in the map's centre.
7. With all the questions answered, it's time to sit back and reflect on what you have discovered.
8. Consider what you will take from the empathy map to inform your engagement with the person or organisation you have mapped. You now have a much better understanding of their drivers and needs — very cool!

Think & Feel
Who & what do they believe?
Who & what do they trust?
Who & what worries them?
Who & what makes them comfortable?

Listen
Who & what do they listen to?
Who & what don't they listen to?
Who & what do they have to listen to?

Gain
What do they want to achieve
Do they want to take incremental steps?
Do they want big wins quickly?
For whom do they wish to make gains?

Pain
Who & what frustrates them?
Who & what challenges them?
What are their concerns?
What are their fears?

See
Who & what do they see
in their environment?

Who & what do they not
see in their environment?

Say & Do
What do they say?
What do they do?
What are their responsibilities?

---

* Hansard documents the proceedings of parliament and parliamentary committees. Each government has a Hansard.

Your turn — empathy mapping activity

I want you to identify one person and one organisation to empathy map. Follow the eight empathy mapping steps above. That's it!

The checklist for change

It's fitting that this last chapter of *Rollercoaster* has two checklists for change. The first, your personal checklist, covers your:

1. assumptions
2. biases
3. expertise.

The second is the checklist for policy change, covering:

1. the *now* — the starting point
2. the *what good looks like* — the end point
3. the *change* — what happens between the *now* and the *what good looks like*.

The checklists for change are your starting point. My expectation is that you will:

1. Complete your personal checklist at the beginning of each policy development.
2. Have a policy change checklist for each policy you work on.
3. Determine what works best for you and your team — one (longer) checklist for policy change, or three separate though related checklists.
4. Gain full advantage from your personal checklists by:
   a. being honest about your biases and assumptions

     b.   acknowledging how your expertise grows with every policy and celebrating how you are becoming a *bloody good* policy officer.

5.   Gain full advantage from your policy change checklists by:

     a.   including links/references to associated documents

     b.   capturing your stakeholders' engagement

     c.   completing, updating and reviewing your checklist in a timely manner

     d.   using your checklist to inform other processes — reviews, monitoring and evaluation, briefs, updates, traffic light reports (aka GAR reports – red, amber, green) (we will use a traffic light system in our 'mother' checklist for change)

     e.   keeping your checklist for change at the top of your policy kitbag so that you know exactly where a policy is at, at any time, night or day.

Below are *Rollercoaster*'s checklists for change.

Your turn — checklist for change activity

I think you know how this works now! So jump in straight away. First make your personal checklist and then make the checklist for policy change — for you, your team and those who will be impacted by a policy or by its absence.

Do let me know what changes you make to either or both checklists — I love learning new things.

Over to you.

PERSONAL CHECKLIST

MY NAME: POLICY NAME:

	Responsible officer for the policy development	My role and tasks	Policy development start date	Policy development end date
POLICY OVERVIEW				
	Clarity of policy purpose — why is it needed?			
	Clarity of policy purpose — what will it do?			
	Clarity of policy purpose — who will be impacted by it or by its absence?			

DATE:

Expected inter- and intra- dependencies	Anticipated stakeholders	Anticipated research scope	Status
	List individuals and organisations across relevant sectors	*All documentation associated with the specific task, i.e., Policy tools Stakeholder engagement & feedback Published research Qualitative & quantitative data Briefs Status updates, etc.*	*Green - on track* **G** *Amber - potential risk(s)* **A** *Red - identified risk(s)* **R**

Rollercoaster

PERSONAL CHECKLIST

MY NAME: POLICY NAME: DATE:

	Detailed responses	Risk of inappropriately influencing a policy's development
MY ASSUMPTIONS	*What are my assumptions relevant to this policy? Where have they come from? Is there any evidence to support them? What will I do to confirm whether my assumptions are founded or not? What controls can I put in place to stop them inappropriately influencing my work?*	*Green - all clear -* **G** *Amber - I need to be careful* **A** *Red - I have to mitigate* **R**
	Assumption: Source of my assumption: Evidence to support my assumption: Controls:	
Add rows to cover all my assumptions		
MY BIASES	*What are my biases relevant to this policy? Where have they come from? Is there any evidence to support them? What will I do to confirm whether my biases are founded or not? What controls can I put in place to stop them inappropriately influencing my work?*	*Green - all clear -* **G** *Amber - I need to be careful* **A** *Red - I have to mitigate* **R**
	Bias: Source of my bias: Evidence to support my bias: Controls:	
Add rows to cover all my biases		
MY POLICY EXERTISE	What do I do well that will benefit this policy development? What opportunities do I have in this policy development to increase my expertise? What opportunities do I have in this policy development to start to learn about a new policy skill that I can add to my policy kitbag?	I can apply this expertise to this policy development ★ ★ ★ I can build my expertise in this area during this policy development ★ ★ This is a great opportunity for me to start to build this expertise ★
	My policy expertise is:	★ ★ ★
	I would like to increase my expertise in this policy skill:	★ ★
	I would like to start to learn about this policy skill:	★
Add rows to cover all my policy expertise | opportunities to increase my expertise | opportunities to learn new policy skills		

CHECKLIST FOR CHANGE

MY NAME: POLICY NAME: DATE:

Task	Assigned to	Start date	End date	Dependent on	Required for	Associated documentation	Status
Brief description of the task	Who is responsible for the task, and what my role is			Does this task need something to happen first before it can be accomplished?	Which task(s) is dependent on this task being completed?	All documentation associated with the specific task is managed, i.e., Policy tools Stakeholder engagement & feedback Published research Qualitative & quantitative data Briefs Status updates, etc.	Green - on track G Amber - potential risk(s) A Red - identified risk(s) R
Clarity of policy purpose — why is it needed now?							
Clarity of policy purpose — what will it change?							
Clarity of policy purpose — who is impacted now by 'its' absence or presence?							
Policy commitment is clear and understood							
Policy value(s) is identified							
Policy commitment, value and change are measurable							

THE NOW

177

Rollercoaster

Task	Assigned to	Start date	End date	Dependent on	Required for	Associated documentation	Status
Possible policy implementers have been identified and engaged							
Commencement of policy evaluation framework including identification of data sources, targets/milestones, metrics and data proxies							
Solution 1 modelling							
Solution 1 now data and desired change data							
Solution 1 testing							
Solution 1 stress-testing							
Solution 1 change metrics							
Solution 1 implementation framework							
Solution 1 evaluation framework							
Solution 1 presentation							
Solution 2 modelling							

WHAT GOOD LOOKS LIKE

Task	Assigned to	Start date	End date	Dependent on	Required for	Associated documentation	Status
Solution 2 now data and desired change data							
Solution 2 testing							
Solution 2 stress testing							
Solution 2 change metrics							
Solution 2 implementation framework							
Solution 2 evaluation framework							
Solution 2 presentation							
Solution 3 modelling							
Solution 3 now data and desired change data							
Solution 3 testing							
Solution 3 stress-testing							
Solution 3 change metrics							
Solution 3 implementation framework							
Solution 3 evaluation framework							
Solution 3 presentation							
Ranking of 3 solutions from preferred to least preferred							

Task	Assigned to	Start date	End date	Dependent on	Required for	Associated documentation	Status
The now — stakeholder engagement: Stakeholder identification Stakeholder ranking Stakeholder engagement type & frequency							
The what good looks like — stakeholder engagement: Stakeholder identification Stakeholder ranking Stakeholder engagement type & frequency							
Crafting the change — stakeholder engagement: Stakeholder identification Stakeholder ranking Stakeholder engagement type & frequency							
Timely updating and review of your checklist for change							

CRAFTING THE CHANGE

Conclusion: Are we there yet?

Come to the edge.
We might fall.
Come to the edge.
It's too high!
COME TO THE EDGE!
And they came,
And he pushed,
And they flew.
Christopher Logue, 2003

Rollercoaster

Do you think you're 'there'? I do — it's time to take a leap of faith.

As I put down my *Rollercoaster* pen, however, I can't help but think of all the things happening right now that are important when developing policy. I considered writing a list, though it would be too long, and I know I wouldn't be able to cover everything.

So I have one final mission for you — keep your eyes and ears out for shifts in language and who is saying what. Language reflects what's happening in our world as much as it reflects what is not happening. Language identifies pains and gains. It expresses hope, aspiration and excitement as it will express frustration, anger and despair. Language talks to our heads, hearts and guts. Language is a powerful compass.

Language that sticks out for me right now includes neurodiversity, ableism, pronouns, positive duty, Blak, First Nations people, ceasefire, victim-survivors, gaslighting, cost-of-living, healing, trust, reflection, Country, climate, humanity, hunger, floods, pink elephant, rainbow, care, punching above, hope, republic. I know you will think of even more.

Keep *Rollercoaster* nearby. Make it yours — scribble notes, fold down page corners, keep it in the outside pocket of your policy kitbag. And please let me know how you go — I can't wait to hear from you.

Glossary

ACT: Australian Capital Territory

Administrative Arrangements Order: an AAO lists the government of the day's ministers, departments and corresponding matters they deal with as well as their legislative responsibilities. There is an AAO for each of the nine governments in Australia.

Administrator: represents the unelected constitutional monarch in the NT. **Australia's Governor-General**: the constitutional monarch's representative for Australia and the ACT.

Assembly: all the elected members, representing their constituency or electorate, in a parliament.

Australian Constitution: the foundational document, established by the British Parliament in 1900, that details how Australia is governed and ruled, and how powers are separated between the parliament, executive government and judiciary.

Authorising environment: a term used interchangeably with decision makers, and which refers to those with the authority to make decisions, including determining a policy agenda.

Bi-election: an election for a specific seat or seats that have been vacated during the term of a government. Note an elected member can choose to change party allegiance. While this generates a lot of controversy and therefore media and public interest, it does not trigger a bi-election as the seat is not vacant.

Bill: a draft act of legislation.

Bipartisan support: agreement or cooperation of two political parties that usually oppose each other's policies.

Blue book and the red book: the compilation of incoming briefs. The blue book comprises briefs for a new or returning liberal or coalition government, the red book for a new or returning labor government.

C

Cabinet: the administrative mechanism for the decision-making process of each executive government. It is made up of ministers chosen by the first minister.

Capability: the right policy skill mix, ability and experience.

Capacity: the ability to take on additional policy work.

Caretaker conventions/mode/period: when an election has been called in Australia (at the federal, state or territory level), the relevant government enters what is known as the caretaker period. During this period the government must refrain from implementing major decisions. If a major decision is necessary, for example in response to an emergency, the government in consultation with the opposition may determine a course of action.

Central departments: provide advice and assistance across a range of strategic issues. Commonly, the central departments across all governments include the departments of the first minister, treasury, and attorney-general and justice.

Co-design: actively work with others and different organisations to define problems, to shape solutions, and to test and stress-test the solutions.

Collaboration: actively engaging with others and different organisations to build relationships and partnerships to identify and achieve solutions or best outcomes (refer chapter 12 — design thinking).

Commonwealth of Australia: the federation of the six Australian states and the two Australian self-governing territories.

Constitutional monarch: under the Australian Constitution, the monarch is identified as the head of state (of Australia). At the time of writing, King Charles III is Australia's constitutional monarch.

Consult: is a two-way engagement model. An example is when you seek input regarding a proposed approach to a policy development from subject matter experts.

Controls: preventative measures that reduce the likelihood of a risk occurring, as opposed to a mitigation which is a corrective measure to reduce the severity of a risk that has occurred.

Cth: Commonwealth

D

Decision makers: the individuals within the authorising environment who have the delegation to make decisions, including establishing and implementing the policy agenda of a government or organisation.

Democracy: a system of government by which government members are elected by the public. Democracy also extends to our rights, for example, the right to demonstrate.

Departmental or organisational policy: refer to the entry for policy.

Design thinking: design thinking is a user-centric, five-pronged innovation and ideation process that focusses on solutions rather than problems (refer chapter 12).

Drafters: in *Rollercoaster*, 'drafters' refers to legislative drafters, staff (and sometimes consultants) who are responsible for drafting legislation.

E

Elected parliament: all the members of parliament who, as per the Constitution of Australia, are elected by the people of Australia, or elected by the people of a state and territory.

Empathy maps/mapping: a process to better understand the motivations of others, what influences them, what they most want to happen, what they most fear happening, what their day-to-day looks like.

Empower: when a government hands over the policy development and/or policy implementation reins and policy decision-making, such as to a community group or organisation. In this scenario you might become one of their stakeholders!

Glossary

Evaluation: the process of evaluating the impact and effects of a policy.

Evidence-based: refers to the explicit use of the best evidence to make decisions.

Evidence-informed: refers to the explicit use of the best evidence *and* also includes professional judgement and expertise including lived experience, context and values. Evidence-informed policy practice is what *bloody good* policy officers do.

Executive government: is established by the Australian Constitution and is the elected government, now including Australian as well as state and territory governments. Executive governments (there are nine governments in Australia) have the power to administer laws and carry out the business of government (administrative powers).

F

Federal Government: established by the Australian Constitution as Australia's national government. Also known as the Australian Government, the Commonwealth Government or a blending of naming conventions, for example, the Australian Federal Government.

First Minister (Australia): either a chief minister, premier or prime minister. Collectively, the prime minister, premiers and chief ministers are referred to as the first ministers.

First Nations people: the Aboriginal and Torres Strait Island people of Australia.

Flat and factual: describes advice that is based on informed evidence (not assumptions, or biases).

Frank and fearless: how we provide evidence-based advice regardless of the position or seniority of the person to whom we provide advice.

G

General election: an election to determine all the members of a parliament.

Government policy: policies made by a government, also known as a public policy.

Governor-general: represents, in their jurisdiction, the unelected constitutional monarch (Australia's Governor-General is also the constitutional monarch's representative in the ACT). The constitutional monarch's representative in the NT is the Administrator.

H

Hansard: documents the proceedings of parliament and parliamentary committees. Each government has a Hansard.

I

Implementation: an evidence-based process of translating a policy into practice, action and behavioural change.

Incoming briefs: briefs that are prepared by government departments during a caretaker period for a new or re-elected government. Incoming briefs provide useful information for newly or re-elected ministers.

Incoming government: a newly elected or returning government following an election.

Independent members: members elected to parliament who do not represent any political party.

Influence-interest matrix: a tool to analyse stakeholders by measuring and placing a value on their interest and power, which would determine their level of impact on business decisions. The influence-interest matrix featured in *Rollercoaster* has been tweaked to align to policy development.

Influence/influencers: refers to the ability of an individual, group of people or an organisation to sway an authorising environment's decision making, the policy development process and/or the wider community's response to a policy development.

Inform: a one-way engagement model in which information is provided to stakeholders to meet a specific need, for example, a government will direct its citizens as to how to protect themselves and their belongings in the lead up to, during and following a natural disaster event.

Inputs: the resources (people, budgets, infrastructure, IT, systems — whatever is needed) to make something happen, refer to the sport analogy, chapter 1.

Involve: a two-way engagement though it is unusual for it to be a once-off, such as a survey. Your engagement with those who have lived experience in order to understand what is impacting them and what they see as possible avenues to solve their challenges is an example of involve.

J

Judicature: established by the Australian Constitution and commonly known as the courts (across Australia). The judicature has the power to determine legal disputes (judicial power).

Judiciary: the collective name for all the courts across Australia.

Jurisdiction: each government governs a jurisdiction, be it a state, territory or the whole country.

L

Leadership spill: when a first minister loses their position by a vote of their party's elected parliamentarians.

Legislation: laws made by a federal, state or territory parliament, noting only parliaments have the power under the Australian Constitution to legislate.

Legitimacy and support: as illustrated in the Strategic Triangle (refer chapter 2) — encourages the consideration as to whether a government has the authority to implement a policy and if it can use public money to do so.

LGBTQI+: lesbian, gay, bi, trans, queer, intersex +. Please note there are multiple and changing versions of LGBTQI+.

Logic tree: a practical tool to break down and frame complex problems.

Longitudinal study: when researchers examine the same group of individuals over a long period of time and at scheduled intervals. An example of a longitudinal study is the Dunedin Multidisciplinary

Health & Development Research Unit that commenced its research in 1972 and continues today.

M

Machinery of government (MoG): reflects the strategic and policy priorities of the government of the day. A MoG is how a government and its public service are structured and interconnected, and includes systems, processes, and the allocation of functions and responsibilities between ministers and their departments.

Ministerial brief: a formal written correspondence between a department and its minister. A department may initiate a ministerial brief to advise its minister about a particular issue, and a minister may request a department to prepare a ministerial brief. A ministerial brief may be for noting (to provide advice to keep a minister informed), or it could be for decision making (to present options for a minister to make an informed decision). There are multiple types of ministerial briefs, and it is important you are across them.

Ministry: the elected members of parliament chosen by their first member to have ministerial portfolios.

N

National Cabinet: The Council of Australian Governments established the National Cabinet to respond specifically to Covid-19. National Cabinet continues to meet to consider and respond to matters of national interest. Refer special cabinet chapter 6.

National issues: an issue that impacts all of Australia, for example, climate change.

New funding: additional funding is required for an initiative that has not been earmarked in an existing funding allocation or budget.

NSW: New South Wales

NT: Northern Territory

O

Opposition: the main political party or coalition in parliament that did not win 'the' election.

Ordinary matters: the government-delivered or -funded services and functions that keep a jurisdiction ticking. Ordinary matters are often referred to during a caretaker period as they continue, for example, school bus services and welfare payments.

Outcomes: the desired goal that is achieved by the collective outputs created by the inputs, refer to the sport analogy, chapter 1.

Outputs: outputs are what the inputs create, refer to the sport analogy, chapter 1.

P

Parliament: both a physical place (i.e., the Parliament of Australia, Canberra) and the place where parliamentarians — all elected members of a jurisdiction — work to make and change their relevant jurisdiction's legislation, represent their constituents and keep check on what the government of the day is doing. Please note the Australian Parliament can make laws specific to either the ACT and/or the Territory, which it can't do for the Australian states.

Plebiscite: a vote on an issue of national significance but one that does not affect the Australian Constitution.

Policy development: is the process of developing policy, as per the instruction of the relevant authorising environment, and the key function of policy officers as defined below.

Policy ecosystem maps/mapping: an activity very similar to a mind map or a brainstorm activity in which everything we know about a policy is captured (very messily) on a whiteboard (or two).

Policy makers: the people with the authority to determine the policy agenda of a government or organisation; also referred to as the authorising environment or decision makers.

Policy officers: staff who broadly (there will be differences and nuances across job descriptions, sectors and organisation types) have the responsibility to develop, review, amend and rescind policies relevant to the sector in which they work.

Policy: a change that takes people (or people and things) from where they are now, to where an organisation or a government wants them to be. There are four types of policy as per the below.

Operational policy: details how a role, function, task or procedure should be carried out or delivered. Also known as procedures, standard operating procedures, processes, standing orders and standards, to name a few.

Organisational aka departmental policy: supports organisations and government departments to achieve their strategic policy(ies) by establishing their respective operating environment's culture, norms and practices. It's all about what an organisation or department does and how it goes about doing it.

Public policy: a government policy (only governments can make public policy), though 'public' won't necessarily be in the title.

Strategic policy: lifts government public policy initiatives from the page into the real world. At a high level, a strategic policy gives the detail behind public policy commitments. Organisations outside of government also have strategic policies (strategic plans) that articulate their high-level purpose and how they will create and drive change.

PPESCTLE: political | people | environmental | social | cultural | technological | legal | economical. Originally known as PESTLE, this is a tool that was developed to better understand business environments. It translates beautifully to a policy environment (refer chapter 11).

Primary research: is research conducted firsthand to generate research data that will inform a peer-reviewed research paper.

Private member: a member of parliament who is of the opposition or an independent member.

Prorogation of parliament: when the governor of Australia, a state or the ACT (and for the NT, the administrator) dissolves the current session of their respective jurisdiction's parliament, usually at the end of the term for which a government was elected.

Public service: comprises the departments and agencies that drive a government's policy objectives. Each government in Australia has its own public service.

Public value creation: articulates how a policy will create public value. For example, the Victorian Government has established a suite of permanent water saving rules for householders to implement to assist in achieving efficient water use.

Q

Qld: Queensland

R

Real-time evaluation: is an evaluation method that provides immediate (real-time) feedback, for example, 24-hour rainfalls.

Red book: refer blue book.

Referendum: a national vote about a question to change the Australian Constitution. Voters have one choice — to vote yes or to vote no.

Regulation: the administration of any law or rule that is put in place by a government. By default, a regulation includes compliance — there are established expectations about who is required to comply with a law or rule and what that compliance looks like, that is, what people are expected to do and not do. Regulations are delegated laws (sometimes referred to as subordinate legislation), meaning a parliament has given a minister, a department or agency, or others the authority to administer a law or rule.

Representative government: the party or coalition elected to govern a jurisdiction (in plain English — they won).

Representative parliament: all parliamentarians are elected to parliament by voting-age Australians.

Rule of law: the principle that everyone — regardless of status, organisations and all tiers of government — is ruled by and answerable to the same laws.

S

SA: South Australia

Secondary research: is a method of research that involves compiling, analysing and synthesising existing reputable data sources. Secondary research is often referred to as desktop research.

Separation of powers: the division of powers, under the Constitution of Australia, between the legislature (the parliament), the executive government (the government) and the judiciary (the courts).

Shadow governments and shadow ministers (aka the opposition): elected members of a parliament who form the opposition government. The shadow government's and shadow ministers' roles are to closely observe and scrutinise the government and ministers of the day.

Shareholder: someone who owns shares in a company. A shareholder has voting rights in the management of a company, and they will also receive part of a company's profit.

Social fabric: how a society is structured through its morals, conventions, religions, cultures, connections, interconnections, recognition, disparities and exclusions. Different societies will have different social fabrics. Social fabrics can change over time and between generations.

Solution deconstruction: a tool to deconstruct solutions from every possible angle to test and stress test whether a solution or solutions can work and to identify where there are risks of failure.

Special cabinets: a cabinet established by a first minister to be the key decision-making body for a specific issue or issues. A special cabinet is additional to a government's cabinet.

Spill and fill: when public servant positions are declared vacant and new positions are created and advertised. So whether a public servant has been in their job for a long time or just started, if they want to be considered for one of the new positions, they will need to apply.

Stakeholder: is a broad term that captures individuals, groups of individuals and organisations who are relevant to a policy development, i.e., they will be impacted by it in some way, or they may be critical to its development and decision making. Stakeholders can include other government departments, organisations and businesses outside of government, people responsible for implementation and other policy areas. Even a government and its ministers could be grouped under a stakeholder banner.

Stakeholder interest: either generated by a desire to see a policy 'get over the line' or to make sure a policy doesn't get even close to the line. Sometimes interest will be from the perspective that investment in one policy risks diluting the investment in another.

Statutory authority: can either refer to the statutory authority that a regulator has, or it can reference a government agency that is the statutory authority.

Storylining: a tool to communicate the most efficiently and effectively with an array of different stakeholders.

Strategic policy: refer to policy.

Strategic triangle: developed by Mark Moore, a theoretical model that presents three key thresholds to underpin policy development (refer chapter 2).

T

Tas: Tasmania

Terra nullius: Latin for "land belonging to nobody". In 1992 the High Court of Australia found the British Parliament's declaration of terra nullius was legal fiction — an assumption that purports to or does conceal, alter or modify a fact or rule of the law. However, the lived experience that continues to this day for Aboriginal and Torres Strait Islander people was the unconscionable dispossession of their lands, seas and waterways.

Traffic light report (aka a GAR (green, amber, red) report): a visual report that uses a traffic light system — green, amber, red — to indicate whether an entire policy development or components of it are on track (green), of concern (amber), or at risk (red). Traffic light and GAR reports can be used for a range of purposes, for example implementation, project development and delivery.

Truth to power: the courage we sometimes need to provide flat and factual and frank and fearless advice.

V

Vic: Victoria

W

WA: Western Australia

Westminster system: a system of parliamentary government and its systems, developed in England, by which several countries including Australia are run. The Westminster system differs from other government systems, for example, the United States' presidential system and France's semi-presidential system.

Wicked policy problem: a policy problem that has extraordinarily complex, complicated and intractable problems. These types of policy problems are difficult to define and are particularly difficult to resolve.

Acknowledgements

Now that *Rollercoaster* is ready to go out into the world, I truly understand why acknowledgements are such an important part of a book. Right up until I started writing the book, I would never pay attention to the acknowledgement page — is this something you do too? Though get this: writing a book has an uncanny resemblance to policy development. As we know, to be a *bloody good* policy officer and to do *bloody good* policy work, there are not only so many different and moving parts, but there are also so many different people who are part of and influence each and every policy development. And our policy work is so much richer for them, as is *Rollercoaster*. I get many of you will still flip past this section, and that's okay. This is my letter of gratitude, admiration and respect to those who helped me get to this point and to those of you who have been with me long before the seeds of *Rollercoaster* had been planted.

I shared my first attempt at writing this book with Dr Maggie Jamieson, Dr Jo Baulderstone and Kirsty Clark. These three wonderful women each provided sage and firm counsel that led to me engaging a book coach. Enter the fabulous Kylie Zeal into my life. Kylie, you shook me up in all the right ways, and I thank you for your valuable structure, guidance, focus and friendship.

Kylie led me to Jessica Andersen who took over the editing ropes. Jessica, like Kylie, you're not one to mince words, and you were just what I needed — eagle eye for detail and fabulous to work with to boot. You kept me going particularly as I neared the end and was seriously running out of puff. Merci infiniment.

E, aka Dr Elizabeth Ganter, your guidance and friendship helped shaped *Rollercoaster,* and I will remain eternally grateful that you re-introduced me to parallel grammar.

Kate Stead, from Old Mate Media, thank you for leading me through all the other things you need to consider when writing a book — publishing planning, ISBNs, layout, paper weights, trim size, marketing strategies and so much more — goodness, there is a lot!

It would be impossible for me to list all the people with whom I have worked, be they someone I worked for, colleagues and the many people in my different policy teams. You all taught me something, in fact many things, that are part of this book. I carry your lessons with me. And of course there are 10 of you in the de-identified cameos; I wonder if you will recognise yourselves.

To the people who throughout my policy career have generously shared their time, knowledge, wisdom and experience either in a policy working group, policy workshops and the multiple responses to surveys and submissions, I thank you deeply. You are with the non-government organisations, the Aboriginal Community Controlled Sector, the private sector, community organisations, academics and researchers. You taught me some of the toughest lessons and the power of doing things together — particularly the really tough stuff. Your lessons are embedded in my policy practice.

To Stephanie Carter, Doug Lovegrove, Penny Tsoutas and Madeleine Legge, thank you for thinking about what useful content for a policy book would be — and not be! I hope I have appropriately captured your advice.

Acknowledgements

A special thank-you to my beta readers — Kate Robertson, Jenna Dennison, Professor Sam Abbato, Robert McIntosh, Moe Pourkarim, Des Crowe and Thomas Cohen. It was scary sharing my book with you, and I'm so grateful that I did. *Rollercoaster* is much better for it.

To the wonderful people who agreed to write a testimonial for *Rollercoaster* — a huge thank-you. You all gave so much of your time not only in reading the book but also in crafting your very generous words of support. I am overwhelmed by your kindness. Thank you to Jodeen Carney, Dr Lorraine Cherney, Dr Maggie Jamieson, Craig Kelly, Cristina Da Silva-Cruz, Annette Gillanders, Chris Capper, Dr Ben Scambary, Lidia Di Lembo, Nicole O'Reilly, Professor Ruth Wallace and Ali West.

My heartfelt thanks to Mick Gooda who penned the foreword. *Rollercoaster* is blessed to have you at its bow as I am blessed to have you as a mentor and friend.

Alice Cohen, your design work for the cover and throughout *Rollercoaster* is sensational.

To Jean, Tom and Alice, thank you for everything — I couldn't have done this without your unfailing support and encouragement.

And finally, Suki. Thank you for hanging out with me so loyally during every moment of *Rollercoaster*.

About the Author

Salli Cohen is a policy expert based in Darwin, Australia. Following 20+ years in the Northern Territory Public Sector working with state, territory, Australian Government and international governments, for purpose, Aboriginal Community Controlled and the private sectors, Salli established her own business, The Policy Room, with the goal to enhance individual and team policy capacity and capability. She regularly shares her knowledge through coaching and volunteer mentoring.

Salli's experience encompasses public, strategic, organisational and operational policy, strategic development and engagement, driving organisational and cultural change, capacity building, front-line service delivery, and complex problem solving and negotiation. Salli is driven by identifying solutions for positive change, fostering safe, engaging and productive work environments and creating opportunities for people to enhance their policy craft. Her experience is supported by a Master of Criminology and Criminal Justice, Griffith University, and an Executive Master of Public Administration, ANZSOG and the Charles Darwin University.

She is the chair of the ANZSOG NT Chapter, a member of the National Regulators Community of Practice NT and a member of IPAA NT.

Notes

Acknowledgement of Country

[1] Davis M & Williams G 2021, Everything You Need to Know about the Uluru Statement from the Heart (Sydney: NewSouth Publishing)

Introduction

[1] 'The 70-20-10 Rule for Leadership Development'. CCL, https://www.ccl.org/articles/leading-effectively-articles/70-20-10-rule

Chapter 1

[1] State of Queensland, Department of Environment and Science 2023, Koala Conservation Policy, https://environment.des.qld.gov.au/__data/assets/pdf_file/0017/309032/state-gov-si-koala-conservation-policy.pdf

[2] Australian Government, Great Barrier Reef Marine Park Authority 2018, Cruise Ship Operations within the Great Barrier Reef Policy, https://elibrary.gbrmpa.gov.au/jspui/bitstream/11017/3337/1/v3-Cruise-Ship-Operations-within-the-GBR.pdf

[3] Sport Integrity Australia n.d., Competition Manipulation and Sport Wagering Policy, https://www.sportintegrity.gov.au/sites/default/files/SIA_NIF_COMPETITION MANIPULATION SPORTS WAGERING_WEB.pdf

[4] Cancer Council n.d., Slip, Slop, Slap, Seek, Slide, https://www.cancer.org.au/cancer-information/causes-and-prevention/sun-safety/campaigns-and-events/slip-slop-slap-seek-slide

[5] Mackellar D 1904–1908, My Country, https://www.dorotheamackellar.com.au/my-country/

[6] Irving J, Beer A, Weller S & Barnes T 2022, Plant Closures in Australia's automotive industry: continuity and change, https://www.tandfonline.com/doi/full/10.1080/21681376.2021.2016071

[7] Idem

[8] Zhao Y and Dempsey K 2006, Causes of inequality in life expectancy between Indigenous and non-Indigenous people in the Northern Territory, 1981–2000: a decomposition analysis, Medical Journal of Australia, https://www.mja.com.au/journal/2006/184/10/causes-inequality-life-expectancy-between-indigenous-and-non-indigenous-people

[9] Australian Government, Treasury n.d., Key Observations and Overview, https://treasury.gov.au/sites/default/files/2021-02/p2020-100554-ud00b_key_obs.pdf

[10] Department of Industry, Science and Resources, 2022, Robotics and automation on earth and in space roadmap 2021–2030 https://www.industry.gov.au/publications/robotics-and-automation-earth-and-space-roadmap-2021-2030

Chapter 2

[1] Sport Integrity Australia n.d., Competition Manipulation and Sport Wagering Policy, https://www.sportintegrity.gov.au/resources#toc1

[2] Moore M 1995, Creating Public Value: Strategic Management in Government. 6. Print, Harvard University Press

[3] Pawson H & Lilley D 2022, Managing Access to Social Housing in Australia: Unpacking policy frameworks and service provision outcomes, UNSW Sydney, https://shelternsw.org.au/wp-content/uploads/2022/05/Waithood_paper.pdf

[4] AHURI 2024, What are the different types of homelessness? https://www.ahuri.edu.au/analysis/brief/what-are-different-types-homelessness

[5] Australian Government 2021, National Road Safety Strategy 2021–30, https://www.roadsafety.gov.au/

[6] NSW Government 2024, 'Yeah…NAH' 60" TVC, https://www.transport.nsw.gov.au/roadsafety/resources/marketing-campaigns

[7] Saldana L 2014, 'The stages of implementation completion for evidence-based practice: protocol for a mixed methods study', *Implementation Science*, 9:43, pp. 1–11

Chapter 3

[1] Government of South Australia 2024, Strategic Plan 2024–26, Attorney-General's Department, https://www.agd.sa.gov.au/__data/assets/pdf_file/0019/1038151/AGD-Strategic-Plan-2024-26-v4.pdf

[2] Queensland Government 2023, Strategic Plan 2023–27, Department of the Premier and Cabinet, https://www.premiers.qld.gov.au/publications/categories/plans/strategic-plan/assets/2023-2027/dpc-strategicplan-2023-27.pdf

[3] Government of Western Australia n.d., Towards 2029, Department of Energy, Mines, Industry Regulation and Safety, https://www.demirs.wa.gov.au/sites/default/files/atoms/files/towards-2029-demirs-strategic-plan.pdf

[4] State Government of Victoria n.d., Planning on a Page. Planning Victoria's liveable communities together, https://www.planning.vic.gov.au/__data/assets/pdf_file/0022/650632/planning-on-a-page.pdf

[5] NSW Government 2024, 24-Hour Economy Strategy, https://www.nsw.gov.au/departments-and-agencies/dciths/about-us

[6] Foodbank 2023, National Food Security Strategy, https://www.foodbank.org.au/national-food-security-strategy/?state=sa

[7] Bowls Australia 2022, Bowls Australia's 2022–25 Strategic Plan, https://www.bowls.com.au/about-ba/key-documents/strategic-plan/

[8] AusCycling 2024, United Strategy 2032, https://auscycling.org.au/about/strategy

[9] Government of South Australia, Department for Environment and Water 2024, Policies and Procedures for the South Australian Heritage Council, https://www.environment.sa.gov.au/topics/heritage/sa-heritage-council/policies-and-procedures

[10] Coogee Beach Surf Life Saving Club 2021, Club Honours Policy, https://cbslsc.com.au/wp-content/uploads/2021/08/CB002-Club-Honours-Policy.pdf

Notes

[11] Airbnb 2024, Cancellation policies for your listing, https://www.airbnb.com.au/help/article/475

[12] Floriade 2022, Terms & Conditions, https://floriadeaustralia.com/floriade-terms-conditions/

[13] Australian Government Department of Foreign Affairs and Trade, n.d., Passports, https://www.dfat.gov.au/about-us/our-services/passports#:~:text=The%20Department%20of%20Foreign%20Affairs,passport%20application%20at%20Australia%20Post.

[14] Museum of Old and New Art 2024, Privacy Policy, https://mona.net.au/privacy-policy

[15] Crown Perth 2023, Terms of Entry, https://www.crownperth.com.au/general/policies/terms-of-entry

[16] MCG n.d., Emergency evacuation procedure, https://www.mcg.org.au/about-us/policies/emergency-evacuation-procedures

[17] Play by the Rules 2024, Start to Talk, https://www.playbytherules.net.au/

[18] Arts+ Law, Indigenous Cultural and Intellectual Property (ICIP), https://www.artslaw.com.au/information-sheet/indigenous-cultural-intellectual-property-icip-aitb/#:~:text=ICIP%20rights%20include%20the%20rights,traditional%20laws%20and%20customary%20obligations.

[19] CSIRO n.d., Biosecurity research at ANIC, https://www.csiro.au/en/research/animals/insects/biosecurity-at-ANIC

[20] Tasmanian Government n.d. Annie Greig Dance Scholarship, https://www.arts.tas.gov.au/grants_and_funding/annie_greig_dance_scholarship

[21] Department of State Development, Manufacturing, Infrastructure and Planning n.d., Queensland Craft Brewing Strategy, https://www.statedevelopment.qld.gov.au/__data/assets/pdf_file/0024/32388/craft-beer-strategy.pdf

Chapter 4

[1] *Commonwealth of Australia Constitution Act* (The Constitution) compilation no. 6, date 29 July 1977), https://www.legislation.gov.au/C2004Q00685/latest/text

[2] Parliamentary Education Office and the Australian Government Solicitor Canberra 2022, Australia's Constitution with Overview and Notes by the Australian Government Solicitor, https://www.aph.gov.au/-/media/05_About_Parliament/52_Sen/523_PPP/2023_Australian_Constitution.pdf?la=en&hash=D9117474455DBD5DDAA61E699329B64A598291C1#:~:text=The%20Australian%20Constitution%20was%20then,effect%20on%201%20January%201901.

[3] Parliament of Australia n.d., The Mabo Decision, https://www.aph.gov.au/Visit_Parliament/Art/Stories_and_Histories/The_Mabo_decision

[4] Australian Constitution Centre n.d., Introduction to the Six Principles, https://www.australianconstitutioncentre.org.au/the-six-principles/#:~:text=The%20six%20foundation%20principles%20are,be%20in%20the%20public%20interest.

[5] Nicholson G 2016, Lectures on Northern Territory Public Law, Darwin NT: Law Society Northern Territory.

[6] Wild R and Anderson P 2007, Ampe Akelyernemane Meke Mekarle "Little Children are Sacred Report", https://humanrights.gov.au/sites/default/files/57.4%20%E2%80%9CLittle%20Children%20are%20Sacred%E2%80%9D%20report.pdf

[7] Commonwealth of Australia 2008, Northern Territory Emergency Response: report of the NTER Review Board, https://apo.org.au/sites/default/files/resource-files/2008-10/apo-nid551.PDF

Chapter 5

[1] Australian Government, Public Service Act 1999, https://www.legislation.gov.au/C2004A00538/latest/text

Chapter 6

[1] John Curtin Prime Ministerial Library n.d., The War Cabinet & Advisory War Council, https://john.curtin.edu.au/behindthescenes/cabinet/index.html#:~:text=With%20a%20return%20to%20peace,held%20on%2018%20December%201945.&text=National%20Archives%20of%20Australia%3A%20A5954%2C%201299%2F2%20Photo%202

[2] Burton T 2020, National cabinet creates a new federal model, The Financial Review, https://www.afr.com/politics/federal/national-cabinet-creates-a-new-federal-model-20200318-p54bar

[3] Australian Government 2020, National Cabinet Terms of Reference, https://federation.gov.au/national-cabinet/terms-of-reference

[4] Parliamentary Education Office 2023, What powers does the Governor-General have? https://peo.gov.au/understand-our-parliament/your-questions-on-notice/questions/in-what-instance-in-the-past-has-the-governor-general-used-his-powers

[5] Commonwealth of Australia 2021, National Cabinet Terms of Reference, Federation.gov.au

[6] Parliament of Australia n.d., Cabinet, https://www.aph.gov.au/About_Parliament/House_of_Representatives/Powers_practice_and_procedure/Practice7/HTML/Chapter2/Cabinet#:~:text=The%20group%20of%20Ministers%20known,nor%20by%20any%20other%20law

[7] Ombudsman NSW 2024, In Focus. Machinery of government changes and maladministration risks, https://www.ombo.nsw.gov.au/__data/assets/pdf_file/0010/145000/Machinery-of-government-changes-and-maladministration-risks.pdf

[8] Audit Office of NSW 2021, Machinery of Government Changes, https://www.audit.nsw.gov.au/our-work/reports/machinery-of-government-changes

Chapter 7

[1] NSW Government 2003, Food Act 2003, https://legislation.nsw.gov.au/view/whole/html/inforce/current/act-2003-043#:~:text=An%20Act%20to%20regulate%20the,1989%3B%20and%20for%20other%20purposes.&text=This%20Act%20is%20the%20Food%20Act%202003

Notes

[2] Australian Government Office of Parliamentary Counsel n.d., Drafting, https://www.opc.gov.au/opc-services/drafting#:~:text=OPC%20drafts%20proposed%20laws%20for,a%20range%20of%20subordinate%20legislation.

Chapter 9
[1] Mayle P, Robins A & Walter P 1975, What's Happening to Me, Pam Macmillan Australia

Chapter 11
[1] McKinsey & Company 2019, How to master the seven-step problem-solving process, https://www.mckinsey.com/capabilities/strategy-and-corporate-finance/our-insights/how-to-master-the-seven-step-problem-solving-process

[2] The Greens 2022, Free Education for Life, https://greens.org.au/platform/education

[3] Please note I have only taken the policy headline for the purpose of this activity. The Australian Greens provided far more information in their 2022 Election manifesto.

[4] Idem

[5] Buzan T & Buzan B 1993, The Mind Map Book: how to use radiant thinking to maximize your brain's untapped potential, New York: Plume

[6] Marx-Wolf H 2018, Living plants, dead animals, and other matters: embryos and demons in Porphyry of Tyre, Preternature, vol 7, no 1, pp. 1-26

[7] Victorian Government 2020, Local Government Act 2020, https://www.legislation.vic.gov.au/in-force/acts/local-government-act-2020/003

[8] PESTLEanalysis Team 2017, Who Invented PEST Analysis and Why It Matters, https://pestleanalysis.com/who-invented-pest-analysis/

[9] toolshero 2023, PEST Analysis explained, https://www.toolshero.com/marketing/pest-analysis/

[10] Idem

[11] Gascoyne Gateway Ltd 2021, Pre-Budget Submission 2021–22, https://treasury.gov.au/2021-22-pre-budget-submissions

[12] Protect Ningaloo 2023, Save Exmouth Gulf, https://www.protectningaloo.org.au/deepwaterportthreat/

[13] WA Government 2024, Exmouth Gulf Taskforce, https://www.wa.gov.au/service/environment/environmental-impact-assessment/exmouth-gulf-taskforce

Chapter 12
[1] Dam R F & Siang T Y 2022, The History of Design Thinking, https://www.interaction-design.org/literature/article/design-thinking-get-a-quick-overview-of-the-history#:~:text=Cognitive%20scientist%20and%20Nobel%20Prize,as%20principles%20of%20design%20thinking.

[2] Qualser R M & Pandey S K 2022, Design thinking enabling innovation: a literature review, https://www.tandfonline.com/doi/abs/10.1080/13511610.2023.2238910

[3] Australian Policy and History 2022, Can 'wicked' policy problems be successfully tackled

over time?, https://aph.org.au/2022/05/can-wicked-policy-problems-be-successfully-tackled-over-time/

[4] Lawlor L 2006, Jacques Derrida, Stanford Encyclopedia of Philosophy, https://plato.stanford.edu/entries/derrida/

[5] Shepherd T G 2018, Storylines: an alternate approach to representing uncertainty in physical aspects of climate change, Climatic Change 151, 555–571 (2018), https://doi.org/10.1007/s10584-018-2317-9

[6] Stanley D & Castles G 2019, The So What Strategy, Clarity Know How Pty Ltd

[7] Department of the Prime Minister and Cabinet, Australian Government n.d., Closing the Gap. Joint Council on Closing the Gap, https://www.closingthegap.gov.au/joint-council-closing-gap

[8] Green C H & Howe A P n.d., The Trust Equation, https://trustedadvisor.com/why-trust-matters/understanding-trust/understanding-the-trust-equation

Chapter 13

[1] Mendelow A 1981, Environmental Scanning — The Impact of the Stakeholder Concept, https://aisel.aisnet.org/cgi/viewcontent.cgi?article=1009&context=icis1981

[2] Mitroff & Mason as cited in Mendelow A 1981, Environmental Scanning — The Impact of the Stakeholder Concept, https://aisel.aisnet.org/cgi/viewcontent.cgi?article=1009&context=icis1981

[3] Inspired by Pink G 2021, Navigating Regulatory Language. An A to Z Guide, RECAP Consultants Pty Ltd, Canberra, Australia

[4] boardmix 2024, Mendelow's Matrix: What is it and how to use it, https://boardmix.com/knowledge/mendelow-s-matrix/#:~:text=The%20matrix%20enables%20businesses%20to,and%20High%20Interest%2DHigh%20Influence.

[5] MindTools 2024, Empathy Mapping, https://www.mindtools.com/abtn3bi/empathy-mapping

It's over to you now

Keep *Rollercoaster* at the top of your policy kitbag, share it with others and make it your own by scribbling all over it. Most importantly, take pride in your policy craft. You are part of an extraordinary group of people across the country working hard to make things better.

It's time for you to fly.

Remember you can DM me on
LinkedIn: https://www.linkedin.com/in/salli-cohen-the-policy-room/
or email me: sallicohen@thepolicyroom.com

And don't forget to download the tables - get them from my website via the QR code:

www.ingramcontent.com/pod-product-compliance
Lightning Source LLC
Chambersburg PA
CBHW042346030426

42335CB00031B/3470